Inclusive Practice
in the Early Years

Behavioural, Emotional and Social Difficulties

Supporting Special Needs in the Early Years Foundation Stage

Dr Hannah Mortimer

Ages
3–5

Author
Dr Hannah Mortimer

Editor
Sally Gray

Series Designer
Rebecca Male

Designer
Q2A Media

Illustrations
Debbie Clark

Cover artwork
Rebecca Male

Acknowledgements

Cover artwork © Comstock Inc; Corel Corporation; Digitalstock/Corbis; IIngram Publishing; Jupiter Images; Photodisc Inc/Getty; Stockbyte.
Every effort has been made to trace copyright holders and the publishers apologise for any inadvertent omissions.

Text © 2004, Hannah Mortimer
© 2004, Scholastic Ltd

Designed using Adobe InDesign

Published by Scholastic Ltd, Villiers House,
Clarendon Avenue, Leamington Spa, Warwickshire CV32 5PR

Visit our website at www.scholastic.co.uk

Printed by Bell and Bain Ltd, Glasgow

1 2 3 4 5 6 7 8 9 0 7 8 9 0 1 2 3

British Library Cataloguing-in-Publication Data A catalogue record for this book is available from the British Library.

ISBN 978-0439-94562-2

Behavioural, Emotional and Social Difficulties

Introduction

▲●■ New developments

This new series *Inclusive Practice in Early Years* aims to bring you up to date with what you need to know in order to plan inclusive practice for the children you work with who have special educational needs (SEN) within the Early Years Foundation Stage (EYFS). It builds on the successful *Special Needs in Early Years* Series (Scholastic) in which readers were introduced to their duties under the SEN Code of Practice. In the original series, readers were shown how to plan activities that contributed towards the Early Learning Goals for all the children and yet which also carried specifically targeted learning outcomes for children who have SEN. In this new series the activities are linked to the EYFS and therefore cover a broader age range, from zero to five years. The activity sheets are open-ended so that all colleagues can follow a child's 'play plan' when interacting and supporting a child with a given area of need. This approach is less prescriptive and helps you to tune into the child's needs and use general strategies for supporting all of the child's play and learning, planned or otherwise.

▲●■ About this series

There is a handbook that accompanies the series, the *Inclusive Practice Handbook* which covers all the basic information that you need to know in order to apply the SEN Code of Practice to your setting. Though the Code has not changed since the previous series, there is now new terminology and a greater emphasis on inclusion and disability awareness. This handbook will bring you up to date on the recent changes and help you to see addressing special educational needs in terms of removing barriers and personalising your teaching. There are also three activity books on supporting these areas of special need in the EYFS:

• Behavioural, Emotional and Social Difficulties

• Autistic Spectrum Disorder

• Speech and Language Difficulties

▲●■ Aims of this book

This book will provide a helpful addition to your publications on inclusion and SEN and will be of most use to you if used flexibly and dipped into. It is impossible and inappropriate to provide 'recipe book' approaches for supporting SEN – the aim of this book is to tune you into the particular barriers faced in the EYFS by children who have behavioural, emotional and social difficulties (BESD), providing you with a range of ideas that will help you to plan how you can change what you provide in order to include these children fully. In its widest sense, inclusion is a process of identifying, understanding and breaking down barriers to participation and learning. (This definition was devised by members of the national Early Childhood Forum in 2003.)

> Reflective practice involves thinking carefully about what you are doing and adjusting what you do in the light of your findings.

The activity pages in this new series come in the form of open-ended 'play plans'. Each is focused on an area of play and learning in which a child with BESD is likely to face particular barriers, and each is linked to the EYFS framework. Play plans can be photocopied, adapted and displayed for staff members to refer to on a daily basis.

▲●■ How this book is organised

At the beginning of the book are two chapters which introduce you to this particular area of special educational need. In the first you meet the children concerned. What are behavioural, social and emotional difficulties and how do they affect a child's development and behaviour? Why are behavioural, social and emotional difficulties so closely linked together? Why is it important to use positive approaches and whose job is it to do this? When is a child with these difficulties said to have special educational needs?

The second chapter helps you to understand some of the barriers faced by these children in the EYFS and how you can plan support for them. You will realise how important it is for settings to change, rather than expect sudden changes in the children concerned. The thread of this book is to adopt a social model to learning difficulty rather than a medical model – your role is not to 'fix' something that is wrong within the child, but to identify barriers, personalise learning and teach alternative and more appropriate ways of behaving so that they can participate fully.

▲●■ The activity chapters

There then follow six activity chapters, each focusing on an area of the EYFS in which children with BESD face the most barriers. The following six areas focus upon all parts of a child's personal, social and emotional and language development:

Focus:	Area of learning:
Dispositions and attitudes	PSED
Making relationships	PSED
Sense of community	PSED
Self-confidence and self-esteem	PSED
Language for communication	CLL
Developing imagination and imaginative play	CD

These have been chosen because of the difficulties and differences that children with BESD have in feeling positively about themselves and others, accepting rules and routines, joining in with others, co-operating, working as a group and managing their own discipline. Though the children's difficulties are not confined to these six focus areas, you should develop enough ideas as you go through the book to become sensitive to their needs in other areas so that you can plan your own interventions when appropriate. You will find photocopiable forms and some useful references, resources and organisations listed at the end of the book.

▲ ● ■ Using the assessment sheets

All effective planning flows from assessment and observation, and is subject to monitoring and evaluation. At the beginning of each activity chapter you will find a general introduction to that particular focus of play followed by an assessment sheet. This photocopiable sheet allows you to observe and record what a child with BESD can do at that time in terms of their development within the EYFS framework.

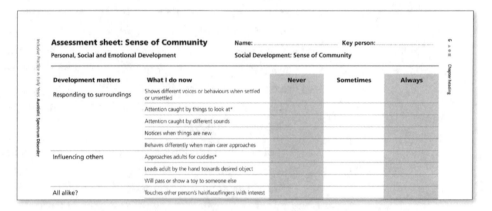

There will clearly be skills and competencies that the child already demonstrates almost all of the time. There will be others that are demonstrated sometimes, depending on the child's mood, who is managing their behaviour and the particular context of the day. There will be others still where the child has not yet demonstrated that behaviour at all. The 'always/sometimes/never' recording method enables you to make a very simple assessment of the starting points for your teaching and support, concentrating on behaviours that the child demonstrates sometimes, though not always. By starting your interventions at the level of 'emergent skills', both you and the child concerned have a greater chance of success and progress.

▲ ● ■ Using the play plans

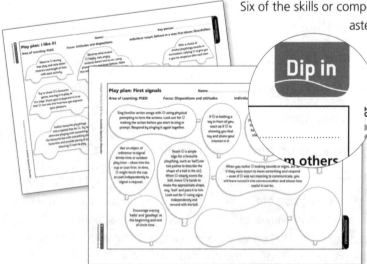

Six of the skills or competencies on each assessment sheet have been asterisked and correspond to 'play plans' that you can adapt and use with the child to support that skill or competency. In this way, you are using the assessment to identify starting points for teaching and support and then selecting a plan that will help you all get started. Some of the play plans can be dipped into in any order to suit your circumstances and some need to be used in a specific order – those that can be dipped into are clearly marked with a 'Dip-In' icon. 'Sequential' plans are numbered in the order of the sequence. Of course, each play plan is written in general terms and you might need to adapt it or even develop your own more personalised plan, depending on the needs of the particular child. For this purpose there is a blank template at the back of the book (page 85). There are also blank spaces within the existing plans to develop your own personalised approaches.

▲ ● ■ Monitoring progress

When you are using the play plans, make use of highlighting to flag up interventions that you wish to focus on, or use dating and initials to record who has applied each intervention and when. You will find a monitoring sheet on page 86 to help you record how your play plan went; what you did, how it worked and what you plan to go on to next. There is also a summary sheet on page 88 to help you record all the interventions that you have been working on, ready for review meetings which will also help you all to plan the child's next individual education plan (IEP). There is further information about SEN monitoring in line with the SEN Code of Practice in the *Inclusive Practice Handbook* also in this series. Monitoring sheets are an excellent way to share progress with parents and carers and you can use the assessment/play plan/monitoring framework as a useful way of involving the family in your interventions. Outside professionals should recognise the steps that you are working through on your assessment sheets and can provide you with more specific and personalised advice if the child you are working with has more specialist needs.

▲ ● ■ Reflective practice

> Reflective practice involves thinking carefully about what you are doing and adjusting what you do in the light of your findings.

In each activity chapter, you will find ideas for how you can observe (to use the 'Look, listen and note' format of the EYFS) and how you can plan effective practice. This way of thinking should already be familiar to you through your knowledge of the EYFS. However, you might not have had previous experience of applying the principles to children who have BESD and the ideas in each activity chapter will show you how to do this. Reflective practice involves thinking carefully about what you are doing and adjusting what you do in the light of your findings. In order to do this in your work with children with BESD, you will need to tune in to their particular needs and what triggers their inappropriate behaviour, learn how you can plan approaches in the light of your discoveries and then evaluate how effective your interventions have been. We hope that you find the format suggested in this series easy to use, effective for the children concerned and a helpful way of developing your reflective practice.

▲ ● ■ Working with others

Find out who else is available in your authority for advising you when you work with children who have BESD. Your local education office (SEN/inclusion section) should be able to advise you. Remember too that the real experts are the parents and carers

themselves. If a child has already been identified as having BESD, make time right at the beginning of your relationship together to let them tell their story and share their interpretation of their child. You will read more about working with others in the *Inclusive Practice Handbook*. Remember that when using paperwork and other communications with parents and carers, it is important to ascertain if there are any translation or literacy concerns to be addressed.

Resources

▲ ● ■ Useful books for adults

- *Effective Intervention in Primary Schools – Nurture Groups*, Second Edition by M. Bennathan and M. Boxhall (David Fulton Publishers).
- *Circle Time for the Very Young* by Margaret Collins (Lucky Duck Publishing Ltd).
- *New Toddler Taming: A Parent's Guide* to the First Four Years by Dr Christopher Green (Vermilion).
- *Social Skills in the Early Years: Supporting Social and Behavioural Learning* by Kay Mathieson (Paul Chapman Publishing).
- *Attention Seeking: A Practical Solution in the Classroom* by Dr Nigel Mellor (Paul Chapman Publishing).
- *Positive Parenting* by Frank Merrett (QEd).
- *An A to Z of Tricky Behaviours in the Early Years*, *Behaviour Management in the Early Years*, *Supporting Children with AD/HD and Attention Difficulties in the Early Years*, *Emotional Literacy and Mental Health in the Early Years* and *Personal, Social and Emotional Development in the Early Years* all by Hannah Mortimer (QEd).
- *Turn Your School Round* and *More Quality Circle Time* by Jenny Mosley (LDA Learning).
- *Here We Go Round – Quality Circle Time for 3–5 Year Olds* by Jenny Mosley and Helen Sonnet (Positive Press Ltd).
- *Young Children's Behaviour*, Second Edition: Practical Approaches for Caregivers and Teachers by Louise Porter (Paul Chapman Publishing).
- *From Pram to Primary – Parenting Small Children from Birth to Age Six or Seven* by Michael and Teri Quinn (Family Caring Trust, www.familycaring.co.uk).
- *Ring of Confidence (A Quality Circle Time Programme to Support Personal Safety for the Foundation Stage)* by Penny Vine and Teresa Todd (Positive Press Ltd).

▲ ● ■ Useful resources and training

- Being Yourself – hand puppets and therapeutic games for professionals working to improve mental wellbeing and emotional literacy in children. Catalogues available from Smallwood Publishing Ltd, The Old Bakery, Charlton House, Dour Street, Dover, Kent CT16 1ED (www.smallwood.co.uk).
- Brainwaves – suppliers of motivating stickers and rewards. Contact: Brainwaves, Bodmin, Cornwall PL31 2RT (www.brainwaves.net).
- Lucky Duck Publishing Ltd – videos, books and resources. Order a catalogue by phone or online: 0117 947 5150; www.luckyduck.co.uk.
- The Magination Press specialises in books which help young children deal with personal or psychological concerns. Send for a catalogue from The Eurospan Group, 3 Henrietta Street, Covent Garden, London WC2E 8LU (www.eurospan.co.uk).
- *Music Makers – Music Circle Times to Include Everyone* by Hannah Mortimer (QEd).
- Persona Doll Training UK – 51 Granville Road, London N12 0JH (www.persona-doll-training.org).
- Super Stickers (for reward and motivation) www.superstickers.com
- 'Understanding Childhood' leaflets available from The Child Psychotherapy Trust. Visit www.childpsychotherapytrust.org.uk for downloadable leaflets or to order a catalogue.
- *Worry Box: Managing Anxiety in Young Children* and *Fireworks: Managing Anger in Young Children*, both by Hannah Mortimer (QEd).

Meet the Children

Each child comes to your group with a unique collection of experiences leading to ways they prefer to be handled, different temperaments and levels of maturity. Children can show behavioural, social or emotional difficulties for many different reasons and will need individual approaches to meet their needs. Your role is to tune into their particular strengths and weaknesses. In this chapter, we meet some children with BESD and consider the information that you would need to gather when planning how to support them.

▲ ● ■ James

James is four. He attends a small village playgroup where staff describe him as 'ruling the roost'. James learns very quickly and has a lively imagination. He is quick to ask questions and to argue the answers, and recently has stopped 'doing as he is nicely asked'. He tends to disrupt other children's play and, unfortunately, has a tendency to choose smaller and less-able children as the brunt of his aggressive play. James loves adult attention and often appears to behave in a way that draws their attention. He has not yet learned how to play sociably in a group, to share or to take turns. He is an only child and has not had the chance to mix with other children except in this playgroup.

▲ ● ■ Sol

Sol is three and is very happy to come to nursery. He has a lot of energy and has not yet learned to settle for long at any one activity. He appears to like being with other children but has as yet no concept of how to take turns or to share. Sol becomes frustrated very quickly and can lash out at the other children or scratch their faces when things do not go his way. He does not appear to realise that he has hurt them and carries on as if nothing has happened. Sol has 'good days' and 'bad days'. Sometimes he appears to need a great deal of support and supervision, crying or throwing a temper tantrum frequently. These episodes appear to coincide with times when he is moving between foster care and home.

▲ ● ■ Jessie

Jessie is three. She attends a Children's Centre each day and is very withdrawn. She clings to her mother when she arrives and then appears to 'freeze', expressing very little emotion for the rest of the session. Jessie rarely initiates play or interaction with others and is very passive. She will comply with requests, though silently. Recently she has begun to play in the home corner on her own, though stops if anyone comes near.

▲ ● ■ All different

Here we have three very different children, each displaying behaviour that is proving challenging for the adults in the group. James is a bright little boy with little experience of socialising who is behaving in the way he knows best to 'keep life interesting'. Sol, in fact, has had many major changes in his short life and has few emotional reserves to call on. He feels insecure and has not yet learned self-control, behaving in the way he does until an adult steps in and stops him. Jessie is a real concern to the adults in her group. Although she never disrupts or hurts the other children, her very passivity and silence mean that she cannot access the EYFS successfully. You will meet these same difficulties and needs again later in the book as you are introduced to the planning and assessment pages.

▲ ● ■ Challenging behaviour

> It falls on us to understand but not to diagnose – to 'tune in' rather than to 'fix a fault' within the child.

When you meet the individual children concerned, you can see immediately how senseless it becomes to talk of 'naughty children' and how much more meaningful it is to refer to 'challenging behaviour' instead. As with any challenge, our role is to come up with a planned intervention that will meet the challenge and to find the best way to help that child access the EYFS. It falls on us to understand but not to diagnose – to 'tune in' rather than to 'fix a fault' within the child. Challenges are rarely easy, and we need to support each other and work closely with parents and carers in the process.

▲ ● ■ What all children are entitled to

It can be a useful exercise to think about the rights and entitlements of all children before you start becoming too involved in what makes a particular child's behaviour difficult or different. What might these rights and entitlements look and feel like from the child's point of view?

• I am entitled to be cared for by a small number of grown-ups who I know well, who are always there for me, who understand me and know what I need.

• I am entitled to opportunities to make friends with lots of other children and adults as well. We should all respect each other as people, even if my behaviour can be really difficult at times. You might have to teach me how to do this by setting me a good example.

• I am entitled to be safe and to know that no-one will harm me here, either physically or emotionally.

• I am entitled to feel good about myself, the group and everyone here. Again, I might need your support to do this as I do not always feel confident or happy about things.

• I am entitled to have my own unique thoughts, feelings and ideas, and to be respected for the choices and decisions I make, even if I might need your help to make new choices and to behave in new ways.

• I should be 'given a chance' when it comes to little responsibilities and jobs within the setting. This helps me to feel good about myself and to learn about being in a group.

• I am entitled to chances to learn through all my senses and through being physically active. I love to move, to fiddle and to touch, and I might need your support to understand this and your help so that I learn through it.

• I am entitled to express my feelings and emotional needs to others. Sometimes these feelings are very strong and rather frightening. I might need your help to express them in a way that doesn't hurt others. I also need you to tell me that it is 'OK' to have such strong feelings and to help me talk about them.

• I am entitled to chances to think, to understand, to ask questions, to learn skills and processes, and to pursue my own interests and concerns. I cannot do this if I am excluded from the group or from others.

▲ ● ■ Creating the right ethos

If you accept this kind of approach, based on entitlements for all children rather than a singling out of 'difficult children', then ways of creating the right ethos develop naturally. Straight away, you can see how isolating a child or preventing them from playing with others are not as desirable as teaching the child how to behave appropriately. It is clear from the entitlements that all children need to be supported in their learning by staff who:

• work with parents and carers with trust, respecting each other's concerns, circumstances, practices and traditions;

• are respectful of differences between individual children;

• provide an environment, indoors and outdoors, that is healthy, interesting, involving, safe, and fun, and which allows children to be physical;

• have high expectations of all children's developing capabilities, giving them opportunities to take risks, to experience success and failure, and to reflect on their own learning and achievements;

• value the children for their religious, ethnic/racial, cultural, linguistic and sex/gender identities, and for their special needs, aptitudes and interests;

• welcome the children's contributions to the group and to the activities;

• sensitively extend the range of each child's responsibilities;

• listen, watch, take time to understand, welcome children's curiosity, follow where children lead, and provide time, space and opportunities for extending children's thinking, imagining and understanding;

• treat everyone with respect and equal concern.

▲ ● ■ Appropriate behaviour

What behaviour are you hoping to encourage in your Early Years setting? If you are going to speak of 'difficult' behaviours, it would be helpful to be clear about the appropriate behaviours you are hoping to encourage in the first place. It is probable that you would like the children to be able:

• to feel motivated and confident enough to develop to their full potential;
• to respect themselves and other people;
• to be able to make friends and gain affection;
• to express their feelings in appropriate ways;
• to 'do as they are nicely asked';
• to learn to take turns and to share;
• to make a useful contribution to the group;
• to develop positive self-esteem.

The EYFS for Personal, Social and Emotional Development describes the goals to aim for by the end of the Foundation Stage. It is useful to keep these goals in mind when developing your approaches for assessing and supporting the children's behaviour in the group. The Framework also describes what you need to do in order to encourage the development of emotionally strong children in your setting.

▲ ● ■ Special educational needs

When would a behavioural, emotional or social difficulty become a special educational need (SEN)? There are some children whose challenging behaviour is part of a wider medical condition, such as attention deficit/hyperactivity disorder (AD/HD) or an autistic spectrum disorder (ASD). For these children you might need to plan approaches that are additional or different to usual, based on your understanding of what it means to have that condition. These children can be

said to have SEN and will require the usual approaches of careful observation and assessment, an Individual Education Plan, regular reviews with parents, and carers and perhaps input from an outside professional, as described in the *Inclusive Practice Handbook* (Scholastic; also in this Series).

However, most of the children with BESD that you will be working with will not have a medical diagnosis or an underlying condition and will be displaying inappropriate behaviour for one or more of a number of reasons. You need to give a child the chance to settle into your routines and style of management before deciding that the child 'has a behaviour problem'. Because you have worked hard to produce the right ethos for appropriate behaviour and emotional happiness, your methods should flow seamlessly from what you would offer to any child to what you offer one who still needed support to be sociable and to settle. Only if you have tried all the usual approaches for encouraging appropriate behaviour over at least a term would you then decide that the child had SEN. At that stage, you would adopt the usual SEN approaches, planning interventions that were 'additional or different' to usual. The decision as to whether to adopt SEN approaches thus becomes a pragmatic one – 'because you need to in order for the child to access the EYFS' rather than 'because there is a problem within the child'.

▲ ● ■ Children whose behaviour is inappropriate

> ...your role is not to diagnose why a child is behaving in that way, but rather to identify what the barriers to progress are and put together a plan to minimise these.

When you take a pragmatic decision about whether to adopt SEN approaches (in partnership with parents and carers) it becomes easier to understand that your role is not to diagnose why a child is behaving in that way, but rather to identify what the barriers to progress are and put together a plan to minimise these. You will find plenty of strategies to call upon in the next chapter, 'Removing the Barriers' (page 17).

Why do children behave in so many different ways? We now believe that this is a combination of their own life experiences (particularly related to their early attachments and their emotional history); the way they have been managed; the opportunities they have had to learn how to behave; and their particular temperaments. Here are some examples of why children might behave inappropriately, even if there is no underlying medical condition:

• Perhaps they have experienced major life changes, separations and losses at the stage when they were developing confidence and attachments and this has left them with emotional difficulties or unusual patterns of attachment.

• Perhaps they have not received consistent handling and containment, and have not yet learned about rules, requests and boundaries.

• Perhaps they have certain temperaments that mean that social exchanges do not flow smoothly for them, and they have not yet learned that one needs to compromise and negotiate.

• Perhaps there has been violence and aggression in their lives and they have learned that this is an effective way to respond.

• Perhaps they are still at a younger stage of their development and have yet to learn the social skills needed to behave appropriately.

• Perhaps they are not eating and drinking healthily, and this is affecting their behaviour and attention.

▲ ● ■ Gathering information

You are likely to find yourself working in one of two situations. Either you are about to welcome a child into your setting who is already known to show behavioural, emotional or social difficulties, or perhaps you are identifying these for the first time. In either case, your first task is to gather what background information you can in order to tune into that child's strengths, weaknesses, needs and barriers. Talking to parents or carers is an obvious starting point, though it is not always easy to raise the issue of behaviour problems. You can do this best by keeping your questions open-ended, for example: 'How much help does he need to do as he's asked?', rather than 'Does he do as he's told?' Keep the tone non-judgmental: 'How does he manage his temper?', rather than 'Your child has behaviour difficulties.' Again, everything becomes so much easier when you set the right tone, showing that you mean to support and not to judge and referring to challenging behaviours and not to children with problems.

▲ ● ■ Asking the right questions

There are certain questions that you could ask of all children when they first join you. At this early stage, you are entitled to be naïve and so your questioning will not be interpreted as prying. For a start, you can ask about the child's history – who they live with, who else is in the family, who will be picking up and collecting. This can sometimes lead on to your finding out about the child's life changes. It is also reasonable to ask whether there are other professionals involved who might be able

to help you get to know the child – certainly there should be a health visitor, and perhaps there will be a family support worker or social worker as well. Otherwise, you can use your early questions to flag up whether you might need to support a child more closely in the group. For example:

• How much experience has she had mixing with other children? How did she manage?

• How much help does he need to concentrate? What will he play at for longest at home?

• Has he learned how to do as he is asked yet? When is he most helpful? When does he need more support?

• Has she had chances to share with other children yet? How is this coming on?

• Tell me something he did that made you feel really proud of him!

• When is she on her best behaviour? What does she enjoy doing?

• When do you find his behaviour most challenging? How do you deal with this at home? What seems to work?

• What are your biggest hopes for her in the group? What behaviour would you like her to learn? Can we work together on this?

▲ ● ■ Making observations

As a next step, you can begin to stand back and make some observations of the child's behaviour. You can do this in several ways:

Diary records

Record incidences of challenging behaviour, but also keep detailed records of the child's strengths so that you have something to build on. Balance 'bad news' with 'good news' as far as you are able.

'Fly on the wall' observations

Arrange for an additional pair of hands while you sit back and observe. Ask colleagues to handle the child's behaviour in the usual way as you write down what you actually see and hear. This will provide you with a wealth of information about the child's strengths and what seemed to lead up to any difficult behaviour. For example, for every child with a 'short fuse', there are often others who know just how to light that fuse!

S.T.A.R. observation

Use the photocopiable observation sheets on pages 90 and 91. One is for you to record incidences of difficult behaviour (page 90) and the other to balance this with recording incidences of impressive (or simply appropriate) behaviour (page 91). These enable you to gather information about: the Setting (what happened before the behaviour took place, the context, the situation at the time); the Trigger (what seemed to set the behaviour off); the Action (exactly what the child did); and the Response (what happened as a result of the behaviour or what those around the child did next). Once you have collected this information over three weeks or so, you will probably begin to see a pattern emerging (see page 23, 'Removing the barriers' for additional information).

Frequency count

If a behaviour is very observable and obvious – such as an attempt to bite or a particular type of temper tantrum, then keep a record of the number of times it happens in each session. This will help you to monitor how effective any intervention is being (bearing in mind that behaviour often becomes worse before it gets better). However, this method will not provide you with the information about the context of the behaviour that you might need in order to understand what you should do about it.

You can also make use of the play plans and assessment sheets incorporated in this book.

Using the play plans and assessment sheets

Within each of the six activity chapters that follow, you will find assessment sheets for working out which skills and competencies the child has already acquired. Each chapter is linked to a focus from one of two EYFS Areas of Learning: Personal, Social and Emotional Development or Communication, Language and Literacy. When completing these assessments for each child, look out for behaviours that are sometimes demonstrated, but not yet always, and work on these as a starting point. You will see that certain skills on each assessment sheet are marked with an asterisk. For these skills, you will find play plans in the pages that follow. If you need to focus on a skill not covered by a play plan, then you can use the photocopiable template at the end of the book (page 85); the activities and strategies in this book should help you to draw up your own. Each play plan contains eight interventions to try and there are also two blank spaces on each play plan for you to add your own personalised interventions. Use a highlighter to flag up those parts of the play plan that you would like colleagues to concentrate on.

▲ ● ■ Monitoring progress

If you have taken the decision with parents and carers that a child needs approaches that are additional and altogether different from your usual ones in order to manage the child's behaviour, then this is tantamount to following SEN approaches. The method of monitoring progress is therefore described in the SEN Code of Practice and you will find what you need to know in the *Inclusive Practice Handbook* (Scholastic; also in this Series).

There will be many other children for whom you are planning a behavioural intervention who might not be on SEN approaches. It still makes sense to monitor their progress regularly with parents and carers, and to share information and progress. This enables you to assess how effective your interventions have been and to plan what you are going to do next – step by small step. Children can also be involved in this monitoring process, as you help them to negotiate what their next targets are going to be and what will happen once they are achieved, making sure that there is a real motivation to succeed.

If you wish to use the play plans for monitoring, use a dating and initialling system to record who did what and when. This can link into progress monitoring sheets which you will find on pages 86 and 88, and which can be shared with parents and carers using the sheet on page 87. The same simple format is followed in all of the activity chapters.

Removing the Barriers

In this chapter you will read about the guiding principles and some of the basic strategies for working with children who have behavioural, emotional and social difficulties. By tailoring your approaches and strategies to each child's individual circumstances you will be helping to remove as many barriers to their early learning as possible.

▲ ● ■ Guiding principles

It helps if you and your colleagues share some basic principles and visions concerning your work with young children's behaviour. Here are some examples.

• We believe that each and every child is entitled to a broad and balanced curriculum delivered within the EYFS framework, regardless of their behaviour.

• We speak of 'difficult behaviour' and not 'difficult children', since all children are a product of their experiences and learning.

• We encourage the children to behave appropriately using positive approaches which encourage their self-esteem.

• We manage the children's behaviour with a proper respect for the children themselves and their parents or carers. We respect their culture, their ethnicity, their language, their religion, their age and their gender. The approaches we use for managing behaviour must be respectful of all children regardless of their gifts, abilities or specific learning needs.

• Behaviour management and the personal, social and emotional education of young children are not two separate, discrete activities. As a consequence, when we work with young children's behaviour, we will attend to their whole development and lives and not only to certain aspects of it.

• We believe in the principle of the 'loving use of power'. Early years educators inevitably have power; this needs to be acknowledged and used lovingly, wisely and well.

• The interests of the child are paramount. Changing their behaviour must enhance their lives, their learning and their development. It must 'work' for the child.

• We also recognise that children will thrive best only if their families thrive and we aim to work in close partnership with families and the community.

▲ ● ■ What BESD mean for you

It is one thing to hold to a set of principles that you believe in firmly in theory, it is quite another to put these into practice! Having a positive approach does help enormously, though you will find it helpful to have a number of strategies that you can dip into and which other practitioners have found to be useful in encouraging appropriate behaviour. Remember that children who have needs that are additional or different to usual, need you to plan additional or different approaches – you cannot simply expect children with BESD to conform to your usual approaches. Therefore holding to your principles involves making positive changes in what you offer to the children concerned.

▲ ● ■ Effective strategies

Below are a number of strategies that have been found to be effective in Early Years settings. Some of the strategies work well in partnership with each other, but as with all matters, an individual approach is necessary for each child. Tuning into and understanding their particular needs will help you to plan strategies that they are likely to respond to, removing as many barriers to their early learning as possible.

Avoiding situations

When you carry out a S.T.A.R. observation (see below and pages 90 and 91), it may become obvious to you that you could alleviate a behaviour problem significantly by avoiding certain situations. For example, you could arrange for the child to miss large-group story time for a while, allowing the child to settle with a helper and a much smaller group in the book corner instead. Do not feel defeated by these avoidance strategies, as they could be a sensible way of 'breaking the cycle' of difficult behaviour and working step by step towards the future when the child will be able to cope in a larger group.

Broken record

Try not to elaborate and explain more and more each time a child does not comply with a direct request. Instead, simply repeat the same instruction over and over – this is known as the broken record technique. There is plenty of time and opportunity at other times to explain why we do things.

Choices

Use the consequences approach to advantage with slightly older children (age four) by offering the child a choice of consequences – 'If you do *this* then this (positive) will happen; and if you do *that* then this (negative) will happen.' This puts the children more in control of their own behaviour.

You can also use choice in all kinds of play activities so that children feel more in control and can assert their personalities and individuality in an appropriate way.

Circle Time

The process of Circle Time involves key skills required of any individual belonging to a social group – awareness (knowing who I am), mastery (knowing what I can do) and social interaction (knowing how I function in the world of others). You can also use circles to deliver the EYFS Framework and you will find that many of the activity suggestions in this book make use of this approach.

Clear rules

Again, your S.T.A.R. analysis (see page 23) might suggest to you that a child has no clear idea of what constitutes appropriate behaviour or that 'a rule is a rule'. Talk together about the rules and then refer to them continually, using the rule-praise-ignore approach, positive feedback and targeted praise (see below). Involve the children themselves in deciding on the group rules – keep them simple and unambiguous and *show* children what to do as well as telling them. A few clear rules chosen with the children are far more effective than a whole raft of them handed down by adults.

Consequences approach

This works especially well with slightly older children. Rather than 'nag', you turn your words around so that the child is encouraged to think of the consequence of the behaviour, rather than the confrontation. 'If you continue to take Tamsin's shoes, there will be no time for any outside play. If you help, we can all go out quickly.'

Count of three

Some children have never learned that when you say something, you mean it and it has to be done. They tend to ignore requests and directions and behave in a certain way until an adult steps in to stop them. Gain the child's attention, issue a clear direction, then give a slow count of 'one – two – three' as you wait for the child to comply. If they do, praise them warmly. If they do not, help them through the direction yourself (for example, leading them towards another child to apologise, or giving them the wherewithal to clean up the mess).

Deep breaths

Anxious, excited, angry or nervous children aged four and above can be taught a simple relaxation approach. Ask them to sit somewhere quiet and encourage them to look in your eyes and breathe at the same rate as you, as you take long steady breaths in and out. Match your breathing to them at first and then slow down. Make your out-breaths slightly longer than your in-breaths, and let your whole bodies relax with the out-breaths. In time, children can learn to do this on their own.

Distraction

When it comes to difficult behaviour, you will already know when the most troublesome times are for your situation. It might be wet days or when another particular child is in as well. Plan ahead for difficult times by distracting all (or some) of the children onto something different before they are likely to misbehave. If children are left 'in a vacuum', they will fill it with their behaviour.

One idea is to have a 'rainy day suitcase' which you fetch out as a novel surprise when you feel that the children need focusing. It is easy to distract very young children from difficult behaviour. For example, rather than nag a one-year-old to climb down when you feel they are unsafe, distract her with something interesting at floor level and help her to climb down safely.

Externalisation

You can separate a child from problem behaviour by appealing to the child to change what their body is doing. For example, ask the fidgety child to tell their hands to lie still or encourage the anxious child to tell their worry box to stop bothering them! There are some useful resources on page 8 to help you work with children who are very anxious or who have a great deal of anger.

Face savers

Usually, you will find it helpful to make sure that 'there is something in it for the child' when you are expecting a change in behaviour. You can use subtle ways of turning the situation round to make it look as if the child made a choice in behaving better – saying to the child 'Thank you for helping'; or telling the other children to 'Watch Megan and you'll see how to do it.' The use of smiley faces and sticker charts are another example of making sure that there is 'something in it for the child' to behave appropriately.

Good role models

You will have worked out that certain children need to play alongside positive role models if they are to learn and behave at their best. You will also have seen how certain combinations of children can lead to disruption! Often this will mean putting children in different groups for different types of activity in order to get the best out of everyone. Make sure that you provide more attention to the children behaving well than to those who misbehave in your group, so that the whole expectation of the group moves towards appropriate behaviour.

Humour

Some children seem to follow a pattern of moving from one confrontation to another. The strategic use of humour can go such a long way to retaining everyone's good will and preventing situations from escalating. Humour can be an effective way to get a message across to certain children, though you should avoid sarcasm at all costs, making sure that you are laughing *with* the child and not at the child's expense.

Incompatible behaviours

Sometimes you can encourage children to display an appropriate behaviour that is opposite to an inappropriate behaviour so that when they are doing the one, they cannot possibly be doing the other! For example, a fidgety child cannot be flicking bricks if he or she is busy holding up your book. The child who rocks on a chair at listening time cannot do so when sitting on a bean bag. The child who is showing everyone else how to replace the musical instruments gently cannot be throwing them carelessly into the rack.

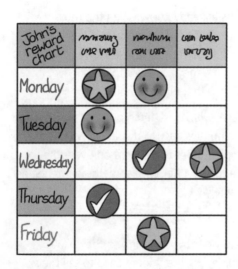

Key person

Appoint a key person to act as a 'secure base' for any vulnerable child, supporting their learning and behaviour and keeping a watchful eye on their emotional needs. This needs to be someone with whom the child relates well. Do accept that personality clashes can happen, and remain flexible when choosing whom the child will play and work with best. To build a strong relationship and ensure consistency, this person needs to be constant for that child over a good period of time.

Motivators

Children are more likely to behave if they are motivated in their play and interactions. There are three main ways of motivating children:

• Make the play activity intrinsically motivating – appeal to any appropriate areas of interest (dinosaurs, sport) when selecting topics, themes and tasks.

• Motivate the children to behave appropriately by selectively targeting and praising positive behaviour. In order to do this, you need to tune yourself into noticing when children with behaviour difficulties behave even 'normally', let alone especially well.

• You can add extra motivators which can be used as tokens for good behaviour – stickers, smiley face stamps, taking the group puppet home, doing a special job of responsibility, a dip into a 'lucky box' and so on.

Nurture corners

Design and set up a nurture corner for emotionally vulnerable children, complete with soft surfaces, gentle music, picture books, sensory play, soft lighting and an available adult ready to offer positive and unconditional time. Have anxious, overloaded or unsettled children withdraw to this corner before problems start to arise from their behaviour. Some children settle best if they can spend time in the nurture corner first or last thing before coping with transitions from one situation to another.

Peer praise

Commending a child who is behaving appropriately, rather than reprimanding the neighbour who is not, can be an effective way of influencing children's behaviour for the better. For example: 'Well done Paul – that is just what I meant. Has anyone else managed yet?'; 'Who's standing straight? Well done, off you go!'

Personal best

Some children may feel that they never compare well to others and success might feel a long way off, or even impossible, for them. Expect their personal best rather than a total improvement, then none of you will be disappointed. Help children with behavioural difficulties to set their own personal best targets and monitor how they feel they are doing.

Positive expectations

Some children behave totally differently in different situations because the expectations on them are different. If you expect a child to fail ('I knew it would be you fighting') rather than to succeed ('In this group we do it this way. Look – I'll help you'), then that is what you are likely to experience. Sometimes when children who have had behaviour problems in one setting move to another, their problems settle almost immediately (perhaps as a result of new expectations, or more experienced and confident staff). Do lean on the experience of others in order to see a child's behaviour in proportion and to share approaches.

Positive feedback

Children with long-standing behaviour problems have often learned to 'switch off' from feedback because it is usually negative. Target your positive feedback directly to the child and make it specific: 'I noticed the way you shared the glitter on your table, well done' or 'I can see you've really thought about this story'. Make sure you have the child's attention as you deliver the praise and use your whole body language, tone of voice and facial expression.

Room management

Rearranging furniture and equipment can dramatically alter behaviour and noise levels, especially if you work in a large community hall. Try to create quiet, focused areas as well as large spaces for movement. Use soft covers, curtains and cushions to absorb sound and make sure you use both your indoor and outdoor environments. Consider too how you use the adults in the room. Perhaps one can take a turn in organising a structured activity whilst the others 'float', providing nurture and support or attending to physical needs.

Rules–ignore–praise

This strategy is helpful for children who you feel are behaving in a certain way in order to 'wind you up'. You can build on the fact that they enjoy your attention, but do so in a way that discourages inappropriate attention-seeking. If you see a child behaving in an inappropriate way, state the rule ('Please put that down'), then ignore their behaviour (if it is safe to do so) and give them praise and attention as soon as they conform.

Self-esteem building

There are certain approaches that you can use in order to promote high self-esteem and confidence in all the children: plan Circle Time activities; appoint a key person for vulnerable children; work in smaller groups to help a child feel less socially 'overloaded' and more secure; plan learning activities which allow you to talk about feelings and about behaviour; and offer children choices in their learning and activities whenever appropriate. Use positive behavioural approaches, praise and encouragement to encourage more appropriate behaviour.

Separate the 'pack'

Certain boisterous behaviour becomes ten times worse when the children are playing in a 'pack' – this is a primitive form of behaviour and predictable in large groups of children. Separating certain 'packs' or rearranging the mix of children in an activity can alter their behaviour significantly, as can planning quieter outdoor areas and teaching cooperative games.

Shaping

When you are moving towards a particularly desirable behaviour for a child (such as being able to share), you cannot expect to get there straight away. Start by accepting even a tiny approximation to that desired behaviour (for example, letting another child have the glitter stick for a brief moment) and praising it. This is called 'shaping', and many behaviours and learning targets lend themselves to this kind of approach.

Social skills training

You will have certain children who you feel are behaving inappropriately because they lack the social skills to do otherwise. The whole means of managing their behaviour has to focus on showing and telling them what to do rather than what not to. Good role models work well, but you will need to help the child to practise the skills as well as watching others.

Sticker charts

Stickers can be used very effectively, either given directly to a child or used with a sticker chart. They work best when they are tied in to specific targets and when they are linked in with an incentive at home. You will find a photocopiable reward chart on page 89. Sticker charts work best for children aged four and over. Always tell a child why they are being offered a sticker and never remove one once given.

Spot praise

Catch the good (or even the 'normal') behaviour and reward it. Children who have just started to show some effort with their behaviour soon give up if this is not noticed.

S.T.A.R. approach

Start by carrying out a S.T.A.R. analysis of difficult behaviour (see 'Meet the children', page 15), gathering information about the:

• Setting – what happened before the behaviour took place, the context, the situation at the time;

• Trigger – what seemed to set the behaviour off;

• Action – exactly what the child did;

• Response – what happened as a result of the behaviour or what those around the child did next.

Then select just one inappropriate behaviour to work on first, one that should be fairly easy to change or one which is causing most disruption. Decide on a hypothesis as to what you think is keeping that behaviour going. You might be right, you might be wrong, but it will give you the opportunity to devise a plan for intervention which you can then evaluate and redesign if you seem to be on the wrong track. Next, draw up a plan to change the S, the T, the A or the R – aiming to move the child towards more appropriate behaviour, step by small step

Targeted praise

Another approach for managing behaviour is to decide with the child what appropriate behaviour you are going to look out for and praise, such as coming quietly to the mat and sitting down at group time. Sometimes you can use a hand signal or a reminder to focus the child onto that behaviour. Make sure you do not miss the appropriate behaviour when it happens, praising it in a specific way ('Thank you for sitting down quietly, Luke'). Recognise that praise must be specific and truly meant – if you use blanket praise, children soon realise that their efforts have not been fully noticed or truly valued.

Time out

This is difficult in a busy group. The idea is to have a 'cooling down' area away from an audience where a child can calm down to the point that you can then discuss their behaviour and agree a way forward. The purpose is not to so much to 'punish' as to 'cool down'. Children should always be supervised and safe, and most groups will have clear guidelines on the use of this approach which you should follow. Seek guidance from an outside professional if you feel that this is the only way forward. Avoid the use of 'naughty chairs' – they reinforce the image of the child as 'the naughty one' and do not support self-esteem or self-control.

Traffic lights

This is a helpful approach for keeping the lid on a whole group. Have a set of traffic lights (invent you own system) and flash up amber as a warning to quieten down and red as a sign for stop. When everyone has quietened down, redirect them again. You can also use the approach individually with a child – 'red' for 'Stop and think', 'amber' for 'What are you going to do instead?' and 'green' for 'Off you go then!'

Transition objects

Some children have genuine difficulty in moving from one area to another – for example, coming from home into the group or entering the large PE hall. By giving them a transfer object (such as something to show a parent or teacher, or a cushion to sit on in group time), you can calm these moments down for them. Giving children a definite job to do in a new situation helps in a similar way (such as giving a message or a package to the new visitor).

Visual timetables

Some children are very strong visual learners but find it hard to focus on what you are saying. These are the children who often benefit from having a clear visual timetable of 'what is happening, when' during the session, so that they can settle into the routine. You can use digital photographs of the children at work and play to make this. Visual timetables can dramatically improve the calmness and behaviour of children who are anxious, children with autistic spectrum difficulties or children with rather chaotic attention spans.

Warnings

Some children find it hard to switch quickly to someone else's agenda. Give a warning before a change in activity (for example, 'It will be tidy up time in five minutes, so finish off now'). Also, give a warning before a reprimand, in order to allow the child to change and save face. In this way, you are teaching them to handle their own behaviour. Some groups have found it helpful to have certain music or a certain song at regular times of the day – for example, for tidying up or for coming over to the snack table.

Whilst reading through these strategies, you might have found yourself picturing certain children with BESD with whom you work. 'Mix and match' the ideas until you find an approach that is tailor-made for each child concerned.

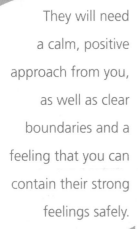

Dispositions and Attitudes

Children who have BESD might need additional support in order to maintain their attention, concentrate and be motivated to play sociably and to learn.

▲ ● ■ Links to Area of Learning

Because children with BESD lack confidence or social skills, or find it hard to behave appropriately, their Personal, Social and Emotional Development is bound to be affected. This chapter focuses on just one part of this Area of Learning, that of how a young child acquires dispositions and develops attitudes to play and early learning.

One of the earliest developmental stages for dispositions and attitudes is the young baby's understanding that they have influence on and are influenced by others. Where early attachments, relationships and care have not worked smoothly or have lacked warmth or consistency, these early influences may have been negative experiences for the children and their behaviour and emotional development can be adversely affected. They might still have a strong exploratory impulse, but lack the sense of boundaries that many of the other children have grown up with. Children learn that they are special through the responses of adults to their individual differences and similarities, and if that unconditional positive regard is absent they grow up lacking a feeling of self-worth and self-confidence.

Your role becomes one of trying to provide that positive regard for the child, whatever their behaviour. They will need a calm, positive approach from you, as well as clear boundaries and a feeling that you can contain their strong feelings safely. They might need you to plan activities that are more motivating than usual in order to help them develop a positive approach to activities and events. They are likely to need a higher level of support if you are going to respond consistently to their behaviour and if they are to develop persistence in their play.

> They will need a calm, positive approach from you, as well as clear boundaries and a feeling that you can contain their strong feelings safely.

▲ ● ■ How to use the play plans

You will find an assessment sheet for working out which skills and competencies the child has already acquired on the next two pages. Look out for behaviours that are sometimes, but not yet always, demonstrated and work on these. On the assessment sheets on pages 26 and 27 you will notice that six skills are marked with an asterisk. On pages 29 to 34 you will find a play plan for each of the six skills marked. If you need to focus on a skill not covered by play plans, then you will find a blank photocopiable sheet on page 85; the activities and strategies in this book should help you to draw up your own. Each play plan contains eight interventions that you could try. Some play plans are designed to be followed in a specific order and are thus numbered and marked **SEQUENTIAL**. Other play plans may be dipped into to suit individual circumstances – these are marked with a **DIP IN** icon. There are also two blank spaces to add your own personalised interventions to each play plan. If you wish to be selective, use a highlighter to flag up those parts of the play plan that you would like colleagues to concentrate on. If you wish to use the play plan for monitoring, use a dating and initialling system to record who did what and when. This can link into your progress monitoring sheets on page 86 and 88 and be shared with parents and carers using the sheet on page 87. This simple format is followed in all of the activity chapters.

Assessment sheet: Dispositions and Attitudes

Name: .... Key person: ....

Personal, Social and Emotional Development Personal Development: Dispositions and Attitudes

Enter date observed

Development matters	What I do now	Never							Sometimes							Always				
Self-awareness	Calm down when an adult comforts me*																			
	Watch other children playing when I am held in your arms																			
	Share a giggle and a laugh																			
	Approach when my name is called																			
	Know what I am good at																			
	Understand social cause and effect																			
	Behave differently when an adult approaches																			
	Repeat a positive action to get an effect from others*																			
	Approach an adult when I need something																			
	Look proud of my achievements																			
	Respond positively to praise*																			
	Draw an adult's attention to something I have done well																			
Social awareness	Play alongside another child without disrupting																			
	Allow an adult to influence my play																			
	Accept familiar group routines																			
	Feel confident in a small group																			
	Feel confident in the large group																			

Likes and dislikes	Show my dislike without hurting others*					
	Indicate choices by using words					
	Able to handle things not going my way*					
Exploration	Happy to explore topics/playthings of my own choosing					
	Tolerant to slight changes in usual routines					
	Willing to accept new experiences with support					
	Confident to explore new topics					
Persistence	Persist in an activity of my own choosing					
	Persist in a structured task of an adult's choosing*					
	Display high levels of involvement in many activities					

Early Learning Goals:

Continue to be interested, excited and motivated to learn.
Be confident to try new activities, initiate ideas and speak in a familiar group.
Maintain attention, concentrate, and sit quietly when appropriate.

▲ ● ■ Look, listen and note

It is helpful for all the children if you look for opportunities to observe their play and early learning and note down how they are progressing. For children who have BESD, here are some particular things to look out for.

• Observe how the child separates from the main parent or carer. It is normal to make a momentary fuss but then to be easily calmed and distracted by new carers. Extreme reactions of distress or passivity could indicate some attachment or emotional difficulties that you will need to compensate for.

• Note how the child responds to other adults and children around them.

• Record how the child expresses feelings – try using digital photographs to record when the child is happy/sad/angry/stressed/bored, and list the behaviours that the child shows in those situations. This will help others to interpret the child's feelings.

• How proud the child is of their own achievements? Are they happy for you to admire and praise, or are they still uncertain of how to handle a positive response from you and other adults? If so, don't give up!

• How does the child respond to anything new? Is confidence a big issue? Do they respond differently in front of different children or adults?

• How easily does the child explore and play freely? Is more adult support and encouragement needed here?

▲ ● ■ Effective practice

• Look for patterns in the child's behaviour so that you can predict the times when extra support might be needed. Use your own methods or diary records or try a S.T.A.R. observation (see, 'Removing the barriers', page 15).

• Make sure that the child has the chance to form a positive and dependable attachment to a key person in the setting. This is especially necessary for children with emotional difficulties, it also allows them to form positive relationships and allows you to apply consistency of handling for children with behavioural difficulties.

• If a new adult or supply worker is joining the group, then use the photographic information (with appropriate consents) about feelings and behaviours to help that person to get to know the child quickly. Make suggestions about interventions that usually work best when the child is feeling certain ways. Ensure that the new adult is fully familiar with your behaviour policies and strategies before they start working with the children.

• Find ways to make each and every child feel a valued member of the group, even where there are severe behaviour difficulties. Support other staff members in remaining positive by reminding yourselves of all the achievements that have been made.

• Teach children to care for equipment and each other. Provide additional support to help them carry that through into action, using targeted praise and showing them what to do as well as telling them.

• Use simple, clear, firm language to direct positive behaviour. Explanations are useful too, but are most effective if they follow later when the situation has been resolved and the child is calmer.

Dip in

Play plan: There, there

Area of Learning: PSED   Focus: Dispositions and Attitudes

Name: ....

Individual target: Calm down when an adult comforts me   Key person: ....

Use gentle stroking and a calming voice as you move together. Sing softly. Persist with the calming cuddles even if ☺ does not seem to be responsive – it may take a long time to prove that cuddles are safe, reassuring and comforting.

Set up a quiet nurture corner [see page 21] for calming children down or for moving to at times of stress or change.

Check for medical complaints or poorly tummies if a baby or child's distress persists.

For older children, make time to follow up distress with a quiet talk together, listening carefully to the child's point of view and offering comfort and advice.

Even at an early stage you might find that some babies are more emotionally reactive than others. Look for what triggers distress and happiness, and make a list to share with colleagues about what actions comfort and calm the baby.

When a baby is distressed, seek to reduce the background stimulation (noise and lights) and go somewhere calm and quiet to rock and calm the baby.

When a baby or child's sobs begin to subside, move to an area where you can use gentle distractions to focus attention – a twisting mobile, a soft toy or some background music.

Offer words for why an older child might be feeling distressed and reassure them that it is OK to have strong feelings, using simple words that the child can understand.

Dip in

Play plan: Look at me!

Area of Learning: PSED   **Focus: Dispositions and Attitudes**   **Individual target: Repeat a positive action to get an effect from others**

Name: ....   Key person: ....

Use puppets and soft toys with ☺ to teach ☺ how to behave well. Make a game of this, making your puppet the 'naughty' one.

Pause to mirror back actions that a baby or young child is making, then cheer or cuddle the baby to provide encouragement.

Use targeted praise which tells ☺ why you are pleased – for example, 'Well done for sitting down!' or 'Thank you for picking that up!'

Use puppet play and role play to reinforce positive behaviour. Link positive behaviour to strong praise and then help ☺ to follow up the new skills learned in the group.

When ☺ has achieved something special – for example, putting on a coat independently, arrange for ☺ to show off at Circle Time and have everyone cheer.

If ☺ has done something very inappropriate, remind ☺ of the rules and then 'take two' as you re-run the behaviour again, this time more appropriately and using targeted praise.

Make sure you spot ☺ behaving appropriately (it doesn't have to be 'extra good') and come in immediately with your warm praise.

For every time you have to correct or redirect ☺, try to find two occasions to praise ☺.

Play plan: Feeling chuffed

Name: ....

Key person: ....

Area of Learning: PSED   Focus: Dispositions and Attitudes

Individual target: Respond positively to praise

Invest time playing one-to-one with ☺ in order to build up a positive relationship. Your praise will then be valued more.

Make sure that your praise is attention-getting and strong – show it in the whole of your body language, tone of voice and the words that you use.

Play games in which ☺ becomes your helper and praises the other children.

Never remove a sticker once given – it is a sign that ☺ did something well at that time. If ☺ rips off the sticker, don't react and keep going with your approach.

Take photographs of what ☺ is doing when you gave your praise and talk through these together later on. You can also mount them in a home-setting diary.

If ☺ does not seem to respond to praise, tell colleagues not to give up – ☺ might not have had enough praise in the past!

Make sure that you give ☺ more attention when you are praising appropriate behaviour than when you are correcting inappropriate behaviour – ☺ might be behaving any old way just to get some kind of attention from you.

Try pairing praise with something more concrete in order to 'kick start' the reward process. For example, give a sticker as well or even a small treat if nothing else works. In time, ☺ will consider your praise a treat and you can fade out the other treats.

Dip in

Play plan: It's OK to say 'No'

Name: ....

Key person: ....

Area of Learning: PSED   Focus: Dispositions and Attitudes

Individual target: Show my dislike without hurting others.

Go for a run outside if ☺ is feeling particularly grumpy about something and try to run off some of the strong feelings.

Spot when ☺ does not enjoy something before ☺ actually loses control – intervene then and there to listen to what is wrong and offer ☺ choices for what to do next that is more appropriate.

Use the traffic light approach – RED ('stop! How are you feeling?'), AMBER ('think what you can do about it') GREEN ('just do it!').

Use puppet play and help ☺ teach the puppet that 'It is OK to say 'No' to Panda, but you mustn't hurt her!'

Set up an angry cushion in a safe corner and encourage ☺ to go and punch away crossness if things feel too much. Never use it as a punishment.

Help ☺ find words for being assertive with other children. Support ☺ as ☺ begins to use words rather than physical actions to sort things out with others.

Use a choice board for the children to plan what they want to do today.

Teach ☺ the gestures or words for yes and no.

Dip in

Play plan: Bad hair day

Name: ....   Key person: ....

Area of Learning: PSED   Focus: Dispositions and Attitudes   Individual target: Able to handle things not going my way

When you are taking turns in a larger group, warn ☺ ahead that it won't be ☺'s turn first time and, if ☺ can sit quietly it will be ☺'s turn first next time. Make sure ☺ doesn't have long to wait!

Try to spot arguments before they escalate. Step in to listen to the problem, offering ☺ new ways of dealing with the situation.

If ☺ becomes easily frustrated when play does not go to plan, teach ☺ to take some big magic breaths then everything will be easier to sort out. Help ☺ to sort out what has gone wrong and then step back again.

Teach a funny phrase to use when things don't go to plan, 'Oh dear! Oh no! We'd better have another go!' This will teach the child that it's very normal to feel cross when things don't go our way.

Sit ☺ near to you during Circle Time so that ☺'s turn during sharing games comes early on. Praise ☺ as you wait for the other children to have a turn.

Teach patience and perseverance by setting enjoyable tasks and making them progressively more challenging, step by small step. Use a sticker chart to record 'stickability'.

Try a very simple turn-taking game such as Picture Lotto with all the cards out. Show that it is first ☺'s turn to win a picture, then your turn to win.

Play with small world items, giving ☺ the role of the person who sorts out problems. Make sure your small world person has plenty of temper tantrums! Use this to talk about problem solving and other people's points of view.

Sequential

Play plan: Seeing it through

Area of Learning: PSED   **Focus: Dispositions and Attitudes**   Name: ....

Individual target: Persist in a structured task of an adult's choosing   Key person: ....

1 Start with a simple short task that ☺ is interested in (such as placing the train shape in the shape board). Present it to ☺ six times, praising as ☺ completes it. Repeat at intervals.

2 Ask ☺ to choose an activity to do with you. As you play together, occasionally ask ☺ to do something simple for you that fits in with the game – such as pushing your train through the tunnel. Praise ☺ for helping. Extend the game by a few minutes each time you play together.

3 Now invite ☺ to join you to do a simple, short task that you have chosen. Again use strong praise and allow ☺ to go and play when the task is done.

4 Continue with this for a week or two, sandwiching short periods of structure with longer periods of structured play.

5 Gradually extend the period of concentration, keeping a note of how each structured play session went. Continue to support and encourage throughout.

6 Choose a more complex task – such as building a tower. Demonstrate first, then challenge ☺ to do it 'all by yourself'. Hold back from encouraging until the job is done. Praise warmly.

7 Continue to provide ☺ with structured play sessions, breaking tasks down for ☺ first and offering support and encouragement between each task. Stay close to watch.

8 As a final step, set up ☺ with a structured activity and then withdraw your attention, asking ☺ to come and tell you when it is finished. Celebrate warmly!

Making Relationships

Because children who have BESD may not show friendly behaviour towards other children and may be difficult for adults to manage, they will need extra support if they are to form positive relationships with others.

▲●■ Links to Area of Learning

Children are born pre-programmed to seek out and secure attention from others and usually this works well for them because their innate sociability leads to close attachments and close relationships. However, there are some children who, for whatever reason, have found themselves craving any sort of attention and, for them, negative attention has always proved better than none at all. These are the children who might need your support if they are to learn social skills, feel safe and secure, learn to trust others, form friendships and develop more flexible and appropriate patterns of behaviour.

Children who have had many adverse changes in their short lives often feel insecure and desperately seek boundaries to their behaviour. They are looking to the adults in their lives to contain their strong feelings and fears. If these boundaries and reassurances are not there for them, then they can present with highly emotional or very 'testing' behaviour. This makes it hard for them to achieve self-control unless the adults who work with them are able to provide the consistency and emotional reassurance that they appear to crave. They might react adversely when you try to challenge and correct their behaviour because they have learned that by 'pushing' they can usually get their own way. They might throw huge temper tantrums because then it will feel as if they are in control of the situation – and they find it too frightening to allow anyone else to be in control. There may be a great deal of anger and fear bound up in their behaviour and reactions (these two emotions are, in fact, closely linked). All this can leave you, the practitioners, feeling confused and emotionally drained. The temptation can be to swing widely in your approaches and attitude to the child, just at the time when your absolute calm and consistency is needed. The play plan suggestions and advice in this chapter will help you to 'stay on track'. Remember to share progress regularly with colleagues so that you support each other as you carry out this emotionally challenging work.

With your patient support, these children will be more likely to achieve those Early Learning Goals that are linked to making relationships. In other words, with your support they may be able to form better relationships with adults and peers. They may also begin to work as part of a group or class, taking turns and sharing fairly. They may begin to understand the need for rules and values, especially within group situations, understanding that these boundaries help us to work and play together in harmony.

▲●■ Assessment records

You will find an assessment record for working out which skills and competencies the child has already acquired on the next two pages. As a starting point, look out for and work on behaviours that are sometimes but not yet always demonstrated.

Remember to share progress regularly with colleagues so that you support each other as you carry out this emotionally challenging work.

Assessment sheet: Making Relationships

Name: .... Key person: ....

Personal, Social and Emotional Development

Social Development: Making Relationships

Development matters	What I do now	Never	Sometimes	Always
			Enter date observed	
Become sociable	Make different cries to signal my different needs			
	Look pleased when others approach nearby			
	Like to be touched or held			
	Watch others without interfering or hurting*			
	Approach an adult for cuddles			
Form attachments	Accept support from my familiar adult			
	Approach an adult for comfort when upset			
	Play happily near other children			
	Play cooperatively with one other child			
	Play cooperatively in a group			
Gain attention in a variety of ways	Look up at you to share something (referential looking)			
	Draw your attention to something appropriate I have done			
	Use my voice (rather than my difficult behaviour) to gain attention			
	Regulate my voice tone (happy voice/cross voice)*			
Seek responses from others	Call to other children to join a game			
	Play 'my turn–your turn' game			

Care for others	Start to use other children's names*
	Adapt how I play to fit in with someone else's game
	Show interest when other children cry
	Let you know if another child is upset
	Attempt to offer comfort to another child
	Help an adult briefly with support
	Join in group responsibilities such as tidying up*
Learning social skills	Pass a toy to another child instead of throwing
	Ask for a toy instead of snatching
	Say 'hello' and 'goodbye' when supported
	Say 'please' and 'thank you' when prompted*
	Enter the group calmly
	Have one or two special friends
Learning simple rules	Take turns with one other child
	Wait my turn at Circle Time
	Handle equipment carefully
	Join a queue and walk in line*
	Know the rules and stick to them 50% of the time
	'Do as I am nicely asked' with support

Early Learning Goals:

Form good relationships with adults and peers.
Work as part of a group or class, taking turns and sharing fairly, understanding that there needs to be agreed values and codes of behaviour for groups of people, including adults and children, to work together harmoniously.

▲ ● ■ Look, listen and note

All children benefit when you carefully observe their progress and plan your next steps around how they are doing. These are the things to look out for in particular when you are observing and monitoring the progress of children who have BESD.

• With young babies, observe their responses as you play with and comfort them. Spend as much time as you can with them individually, cuddling and talking to them, and see if you can encourage them to imitate your smiles and actions.

• Observe whether young children attract your attention when they are doing something positive or when they need your reassurance, rather than just when they have done something inappropriate.

• Is there a noticeable response when other children or babies cry or behave in an angry manner? Does the child seem aware of other children's feelings yet?

• Does the child behave differently in one-to-one/small group/large group situations? Why do you think this might be? Does this help you plan approaches such as teaching new social skills?

• How does the child cope with change and newness? From who does the child seek support and how?

• Are there any occasions yet when the child is willing to take turns and to share? Why do you think these occasions work well? Can anything be learned from this?

▲ ● ■ Effective practice

• It is more important than ever that babies and young children who are emotionally 'at risk' should have one main caregiver within the setting (and, at the most, only one reserve). If changes of staff are necessary, lead up to these gradually through sharing play and gradually changing over.

• With younger children and babies, spend as much time as you can holding, talking and sharing play together one-on-one in order to secure your attachment together. Once the child feels securely attached, that child will be more likely to explore and to learn through play.

• Look for ways of helping the child join in with group activities by planning ahead, securing the right level of support and making sure that the activity suits the ability and interests of the child.

• Stick to a few simple rules and show the children what to do as well as telling them. 'Catch the good' and praise it.

• Establish clear routines and boundaries, and stay calm and assertive at all times.

• Use picture timetables and talking to prepare vulnerable children ahead of any changes in the routine.

• For children who lack confidence, plan opportunities for them to practise new skills or ways of playing in a small group or themed corner before they are expected to join a larger group.

▲ ● ■ How to use the play plans

On pages 39 to 44 you will find six photocopiable play plans for those skills marked with an asterisk on the assessment sheets on pages 36 and 37. Each play plan contains eight interventions that you could try. There are also two blank spaces to add your own personalised interventions to each play plan.

Dip in

Play plan: Hands to myself

Area of Learning: PSED   **Focus: Making Relationships**

Name: ....   Key person: ....

Individual target: Watch others without interfering or hurting

Make a 'hide' out of a large box and watch the other children from it. Talk to ☺ about what they are doing and what ☺ would like to do. Rehearse what ☺ will (and will not) do in order to be friendly.

Help ☺ plan ahead by showing a choice of objects representing what play activities are on offer and then supporting ☺ as you begin to play there.

Start with small groups for free play, gradually increasing the group size as ☺ learns better self-control.

If ☺ is still very young, hold ☺ in your arms and talk as you watch another child play. As they reach or lunge forwards, hold tight and ask, 'Would you like to play too?' Stay close to support.

Use puppet play to explain how all children like to play without being hurt or having their game spoiled by someone else.

Set ☺ the challenge of playing in a friendly manner for one turn of the egg-timer at an activity of ☺'s choosing. Reward with a huge sticker. Gradually build up the time.

Arrange a short play session for older children with two sets of the same equipment. Support ☺ as ☺ plays side by side with another child, patiently returning items to the right child – repeating, 'that's Peter's toy and that's ☺'s toy'.

Give ☺ a cushion to sit on during group time in order to mark out ☺'s physical space. Keep ☺'s hands busy with something to hold if this helps. Sit ☺ close to you so that you can help ☺ to stick to your rules. Praise frequently.

Dip in

Play plan: Voices

Area of Learning: PSED   **Focus: Making Relationships**

Name: ....   Key person: ....

Individual target: Regulate my voice tone (happy voice/cross voice)

Use puppets and soft toys to try out different voices for different purposes. Make your puppet react appropriately and explain how it feels.

Echo back a baby's tone of voice as you 'play' with your voices together – this encourages a baby to repeat different tones of voice.

Pretend to be deaf when ☺ uses a whiney voice, saying that you can only hear happy voices today. Encourage ☺ to try again. Respond positively.

When ☺ needs something from another child, help ☺ to rehearse the 'asking words' and try a friendly voice.

Even when ☺ has learned about different voices, it will be hard for ☺ to remember when ☺ is feeling cross. Look for signs of frustration, remove ☺ from the situation to calm down, then try again with a new voice.

When ☺ is speaking or shouting in a certain tone of voice, add your words to help ☺ link the voice with the feeling. For example 'You sound really cross today. Tell me what has happened.'

Help ☺ to recognise tones of voice in other children and to guess how they might be feeling and why.

Try the photocopiable rhyme on page 93 to practise your different voices together.

Dip in

Play plan: Knowing me, knowing you

Name: ....

Key person: ....

Area of Learning: PSED   Focus: Making Relationships

Individual target: Start to use other children's names

Mount all the children's photographs on a wall and use these to talk with ☺ naming the children and finding positive things to say about each one.

As you watch other children playing together, use their names frequently as you talk to ☺. The aim is to help ☺ become interested in other children as people, rather than as objects to be hurt or pushed aside.

Introduce a persona puppet who has asked if she could sit next to ☺. Ask ☺ to introduce the puppet to all the other children.

Play this circle time game: tell children to roll a ball across the circle to a named child. Continue regularly until each child knows the names of all of their friends.

Give ☺ little responsibilities that will help the other children. For example, 'Can you take this apron to Jack, please?' Say 'Here's your apron, Jack', using your friendly voice.'

With young babies, greet them by name and draw other baby's attentions to each other as they arrive and depart.

Ask ☺ who ☺ would like to play with and then support ☺'s play for a while as ☺ settles in. If necessary, explain to the chosen children that you will stay close so that you can teach ☺ to be friendly.

If ☺ always hurts a certain child, spend time later (when things have calmed down) talking about how that child might be feeling. Use small world play to back this up, using the children's names as you do.

Sequential

Play plan: Tidy up time

Name: .... **Key person:** ....

Area of Learning: PSED **Focus: Making Relationships** **Individual target: Join in group responsibilities such as tidying up**

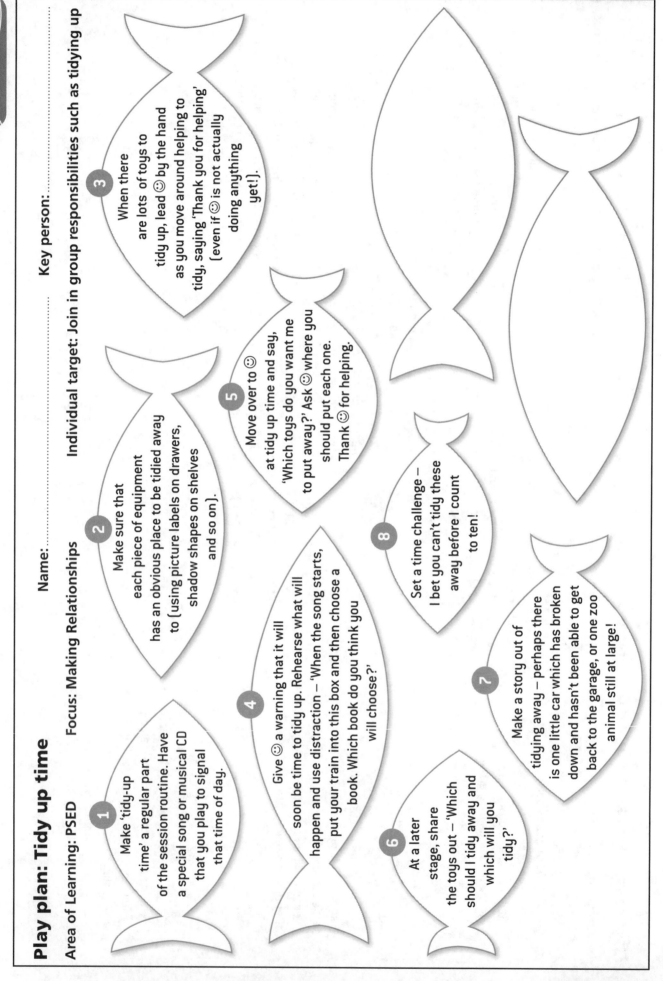

1 Make 'tidy-up time' a regular part of the session routine. Have a special song or musical CD that you play to signal that time of day.

2 Make sure that each piece of equipment has an obvious place to be tidied away to (using picture labels on drawers, shadow shapes on shelves and so on).

3 When there are lots of toys to tidy up, lead ☺ by the hand as you move around helping to tidy, saying 'Thank you for helping' (even if ☺ is not actually doing anything yet!).

4 Give ☺ a warning that it will soon be time to tidy up. Rehearse what will happen and use distraction – 'When the song starts, put your train into this box and then choose a book. Which book do you think you will choose?'

5 Move over to ☺ at tidy up time and say, 'Which toys do you want me to put away?' Ask ☺ where you should put each one. Thank ☺ for helping.

6 At a later stage, share the toys out – 'Which should I tidy away and which will you tidy?'

7 Make a story out of tidying away – perhaps there is one little car which has broken down and hasn't been able to get back to the garage, or one zoo animal still at large!

8 Set a time challenge – I bet you can't tidy these away before I count to ten!

Play plan: Ps and Qs

Name: .... Key person: ....

Area of Learning: PSED   Focus: Making Relationships   Individual target: Say 'please' and 'thank you' when prompted

Set up a themed play area and introduce 'please' and 'thank you' as an important feature of the game – for example, a shop, post office or hairdressing area.

Catch ☺ using the words and present ☺ with a huge sticker – 'I said PLEASE and THANK YOU today!'

If ☺ leaves the words out, simply hold on to what you were about to give ☺ and model the phrase before handing it over. For example, 'Please can I have the crayon...? Thank you, Mrs Dodds.'

At circle time, introduce a persona doll that never says 'please' and 'thank you'. See whether the children notice. Encourage ☺ to tell the doll what to say.

Make sure that all the adults model and exaggerate the words 'please' and 'thank you' during their natural exchanges with the children 'Oh, *thank you*, ☺!'

At a later stage, pause momentarily and expectantly, prompting the first sound, for example, 'p...'. Praise warmly if ☺ completes the word.

Use puppet play to model friendly behaviour including 'please' and 'thank you'.

Introduce a game of 'Simon says' using the word 'please'. For example, 'Simon says stand on one leg, please' (and the children do it) or 'Simon says hop' (and they don't). Substitute the children's own names for 'Simon'.

Sequential

Play plan: Lining up

Name: ....

Key person: ....

Area of Learning: PSED   Focus: Making Relationships

Individual target: Join a queue and walk in line

1 If you are teaching lining up ready for school playtimes, choose a signal you will use, such as a whistle or clap.

2 Use a separate play session to teach ☺ to stop still as soon as you give the signal. Tell ☺ that you will be trying this outside at play time. Hold ☺'s hand as the other children line up.

3 Next, teach ☺ to come to you as soon as you give the signal. Praise warmly and hold ☺'s hand as the other children line up and walk in.

4 As a next step, lead ☺ to join the line and to wait with you while the other children join you.

5 Then ask ☺ to form the front of the line. Give the signal for the others to line up behind ☺. Hold ☺'s hand as you both lead the others inside.

6 Encourage ☺ to go to the line as soon as the whistle goes, and stand still without pushing. Go straight over to join ☺ and hold ☺'s hand as you all walk in.

7 Repeat, but without holding hands. Stay close to encourage and only hold hands if there is a problem.

8 Explain to ☺ that this time you will be watching as ☺ does it 'all by yourself'. Have a big sticker ready and continue to support and encourage for a while longer.

Sense of Community

A sense of community within the group stems from sociable behaviour and sharing pleasure and learning together. For some children with BESD, this can prove a problem and these children will certainly need your additional support.

▲●■ Links to Area of Learning

> Stability in their lives, in their families and in their group setting enables them to make links between the different parts of their life experience.

How do children usually develop a sense of community? As babies begin to respond to different experiences in their environment, they begin to learn that their voices and actions have effects on others. They learn that they have similarities and differences that connect them to, or distinguish them from others and this gradually helps them to form a strong sense of self as being a particular kind of person and belonging to a particular community, such as their family or their setting. Stability in their lives, in their families and in their group setting enables them to make links between the different parts of their life experience. In this way they are able to build up a whole picture of themselves with which they feel comfortable and positive.

You can see immediately where things can go wrong. Children whose early experiences are not warm, consistent and safe, might have discovered early on that their best source of attention from others is negative – only by behaving inappropriately or very physically can they secure attention from their carers. These children grow up seeing themselves as 'naughty' children and behave in ways that fulfil the expectations of their carers – behaving negatively and aggressively. Other children might have experienced many changes in their lives and lack the sense of security that leads to confidence and positive self-identity. These children may shy away from community experiences and withdraw into themselves, having no sense of themselves as sociable and friendly beings.

You might also have met children who have not had experience of mixing with and playing with other children and simply do not know how to do it yet. They may see 'playing' only from a physical point of view, becoming highly excited and tumbling onto the floor in a joyful fight, actually hurting others in the process. These children, too, are going to benefit from your support in encouraging a greater sense of community in which each and every child has the right to be happy, make friends, and not be hurt or upset by anyone else.

Your aim is to look for opportunities to help children understand that people have different needs, views, cultures and beliefs that need to be treated with respect. Through your interventions and support, children should come to understand that they can also expect others to treat their needs, views, cultures and beliefs with respect. They will know that, in your setting, they will be listened to, valued and looked after safely and happily.

▲●■ Assessment records

You will find an assessment record for working out which skills and competencies the child has already acquired on the next two pages. As a starting point, look out for and work on behaviours that are sometimes but not yet always demonstrated.

Assessment sheet: Sense of Community

Name: .... Key person: ....

Personal, Social and Emotional Development

Social Development: Sense of Community

Development matters	What I do now	Never	Sometimes	Always
			Enter date observed	
Responding to surroundings	Show different voices or behaviours when I feel settled or unsettled			
	Show excitement and interest without hurting others			
	Stay calm and interested even if there is background noise			
	Stay calm and settled when other children approach			
	Stay calm and settled in a large group*			
	Behave differently when my main carer approaches			
All alike?	Point to and name photographs of children in the setting			
	Compare playthings with others ('I've got one too!')			
	Notice similarities in clothes with others			
	Accept children's different appearances*			
I belong!	Settle well on arriving			
	Know my own coat/peg/shoes/painting			
	Talk about family photographs			
	Have one or two favourite adults in the group			
	Have one or two favourite playmates in the group			
	Follow the set routine of the group			
	Follow simple directions given to the whole group*			

Remembering links

- Can bring something appropriate from home to play with
- Can bring something from home to share with the group
- Share what happens in the group with family*
- Remember and follow the rules of the group

Meeting new cultures

- Carefully handle and look at new artefacts
- Approach a visitor to the group with appropriate behaviour
- Cope with a group outing with support*

Feeling good

- Am willing to come regularly to the group
- Can choose who to sit next to during Circle Time
- Show pride in my achievements
- Talk about or indicate what I like and don't like*

Early Learning Goals:

Understand that people have different needs, views, culture and beliefs that need to be treated with respect.
Understand that they can expect others to treat their needs, views, cultures and beliefs with respect.

▲ ● ■ Look, listen and note

You need to plan opportunities to observe all the children as they settle and become involved in the group, noting how their sense of community develops. Here are some issues to observe particularly for children who have BESD.

• At first, simply observe how the baby or toddler reacts to the group. How do they settle, what seems to make them happy/angry/anxious? What seems to capture their attention? What seems to upset them?

• Note instances of children drawing upon their experiences beyond their setting, but remember – although this shows a developing sense of community, these experiences may not always be positive. These observations may help you to understand 'where the child is coming from'.

• Note the child's interest in similarities and differences with other children – perhaps what they are wearing or what they look like. However, they may also be interested in imitating inappropriate behaviour in others. You might spot 'herd behaviour' developing early on – children identifying with each other and behaving rather wildly and en masse.

• Note the children's interest in cultural differences and the value they seem to place on them. Children do notice differences, but may be negative about them if they do not understand them, if they fear them or if they have seen negative reactions modelled by others. Try to tease this apart from your observations.

▲ ● ■ Effective practice

• If you spot 'herd behaviour' developing, plan ways of balancing this by encouraging other groupings of children and more focussed and peaceful activity, so that children can develop the sense of themselves as individuals as well as 'members of the gang'.

• For a child who has had many life changes, consider putting together a life story book with photographs of their babyhood, main carers and homes. With the help of parents, carers or social worker, add a simple text and use this to help a child make sense of past experiences.

• Use Persona dolls (see Resources, page 8) to introduce people of different faiths, communities and family make-up. For a child with BESD, arrange for the first introduction to the doll to be during an individual session or in a small group.

• Build on the child's positive experiences and make sure you use photographs and displays to show off any achievements and happy times. Mount these in a way that signals that the child is an important member of your group.

• It is vitally important to form a positive relationship with the child's parents and carers so that the child can see you relating to each other positively. In this way, the child can identify with you both as a member of a family and a member of your setting. Home visits go a long way to helping this sense of dual identity.

▲ ● ■ How to use the play plans

On pages 49-54 you will find six photocopiable play plans for those skills marked with an asterisk on the assessment sheets on pages 46 and 47. Each play plan contains eight interventions that you could try. There are two blank spaces to add your own personalised interventions to each play plan.

Dip in

Play plan: Settling down

Name: ....

Key person: ....

Area of Learning: PSED   Focus: Sense of Community

Individual target: Stay calm and settled in a large group

When you are playing outside, state the rules clearly to ☺ and then use distraction and support to try to help ☺ stay within them. If the rule is broken, give one warning, then bring ☺ inside.

Create a quiet space in one corner or area of the room and withdraw ☺ there before behaviour becomes too wild or aggressive.

Start by playing alongside ☺ with one other child, then invite one or two others to join. Work up to a larger group, taking care not to rush things.

Use cushions, carpets, curtains and beanbags to absorb sound in the baby room – this way the background noise is less likely to unsettle ☺.

If high energy is a problem, try going outside to 'run off some steam' with ☺ before the session. Once you have done this, you will need to 'wind ☺ down again' with a quiet story before ☺ goes off to play.

Divide your large area into smaller spaces using low screens, cupboards and shelving. This will give ☺ the impression of playing in a smaller group. Make sure you can watch ☺ at all times!

Keep in close contact with parents and carers – if they tell you that ☺ has woken up 'in a certain mood', plan smaller group activities for ☺ during that session.

Circle Time is a useful opportunity to get children together in a large group, yet watching them and responding to them as individuals.

Dip in

Play plan: I'm OK, you're OK

Name: ....   Key person: ....

Area of Learning: PSED   Focus: Sense of Community   Individual target: Accept children's different appearances

Spend individual time with anyone ☺ has hurt or upset (and vice versa) to ensure that self-esteem remains intact. Young children can be very sensitive and soon pick up messages about who has more power than anyone else in a setting.

Challenge racial comments directly and firmly, making it very clear what ☺ may and may not say. At a separate time, use the other approaches on this chart to make these comments less likely.

Make a photo frieze of all the children in the group and use this to talk to ☺ about similarities and differences and how we all belong to one group.

Look at your books, your toys, your home corner and your activities: do they represent a wide range of diversity and present positive images? Spend time with ☺ in a small group or individually enjoying this diversity together.

Use Circle Time to find positive things that you would like to say to each other and for teaching sharing and friendship games.

Spend a lot of time physically comforting and sharing pleasure with the babies so that they each see themselves as special and valued.

Use Persona dolls with ☺, either individually or in a small group. These are dolls to which you give a persona such as a particular ethnicity, a disability or a certain way of life or religion. Keep them special and out of general circulation.

If ☺ has been hurtful to another child, deal with it there and then, using your usual rules. However, also revisit the matter later when you can sit quietly together and talk neutrally about differences and feelings.

Sequential

Play plan: Are you receiving me?

Name: .... Key person: ....

Area of Learning: PSED   Focus: Sense of Community   Individual target: Follow simple directions given to the whole group

1 Start by teaching ☺ to stop and look at you when you call ☺'s name. Praise warmly. Continue each of the next stages (below) for a week or so.

2 Find five opportunities per session to call ☺'s name and, when ☺ turns to you, give ☺ some interesting information or a motivating task to do. In other words, make it fun to comply.

3 Warn ☺ ahead that you are going to ask for some help later and that there is a sticker available for good helping. Choose your moment (when ☺ is not too busy) and approach ☺ using name and eye contact. Give a simple instruction and help ☺ to see it through. Reward with a sticker.

4 Find five opportunities per session to give ☺ an instruction. Seek eye contact and use ☺'s name. Give your instruction and then count to three slowly. If ☺ complies, reward with a sticker. If not, lead ☺ through what you want ☺ to do, doing it together.

5 Practise a little task together – for example, fetching the large book to share with the other children. Warn ☺ that it will be ☺'s turn that day to do just that. Secure ☺'s attention in the group before issuing your request.

6 When you are giving a group instruction, repeat it for ☺ if you need to, first gaining eye contact and using ☺'s name.

7 Try passing a Teddy or other object to ☺ during group time to signal that you are about to speak to ☺ and it is ☺'s turn to listen to you.

8 As a final step, secure ☺'s attention before giving the group instruction, and praise warmly for compliance.

Dip in

Play plan: What I did today

Name: ....   Key person: ....

Area of Learning: PSED   Focus: Sense of Community   Individual target: Share what happens in the group with family

Work together with parents or carers so that you can link positive improvements in the setting with a reward from home (such as a special family outing or 'football with Dad').

Give ☺ one thing to take home to show – something ☺ has made or a photograph of something ☺ was engaged in. Tell parents or carers about it to help them to ask the right questions. Emphasise being positive.

Start a home setting diary for the key person to write in every day. This works for all ages. Put in what ☺ has done, what ☺ enjoyed and anything new ☺ has learned today. Don't wait until there are problems to report!

Help ☺ to collect a treasure box of 'keep-for-evers'. For babies, this would include photographs of 'golden moments'. For older children, it would contain creations that ☺ has created in the setting.

Use a home plan to share activities between home and setting (page 87), perhaps working on the same difficult behaviour in both situations.

Invite ☺'s carers to visit you. If this is not possible, try to visit ☺'s home, taking items to share with ☺'s help. Model how to praise and be positive, explaining how this will lead to better behaviour.

As you begin to see progress in ☺'s behaviour, share the approaches with ☺'s parents or carers so that they can encourage the same standard of behaviour and set the same boundaries at home.

Use a child-held camera to help ☺ make a booklet all about a day in your setting, sharing this with parents and carers when it is complete. Add ☺'s own words.

Sequential

Play plan: Out and about

Name: ....

Key person: ....

Area of Learning: PSED   Focus: Sense of Community

Individual target: Cope with a group outing with support

1 Before any outing, carry out your usual risk assessment and have it approved by the manager or head teacher. Be realistic about risks, but also be creative about how you can remove barriers.

2 Always plan a 'safety net'. This might involve identifying what would happen if ☺ had to be taken home from the outing. Agree it with all concerned.

3 Try to make the visit yourself first so that you can visualise where ☺ will find it easy to behave and where the danger points are. Plan your level of support and itinerary accordingly.

4 Keep it simple – if this is ☺'s first trip, it would be helpful if it was not too long and could end on a successful note.

5 Rehearse with ☺ where you will be going and what you will be doing. Repeat the group rules and explain the consequences of breaking these – this might involve having to hold hands at certain stages.

6 Make sure you have plenty of adult support, and plan groups of children carefully so as to make use of firm supervision and good role models.

7 Use distraction frequently on the visit, to keep ☺ interested but not over-excited. Use your expectations and assumed confidence to convey the message that ☺ can behave and enjoy the trip.

8 Make sure that there is something structured to focus attention during the bus journeys – perhaps a book to share or an activity to enjoy with a helper.

Dip in

Play plan: I like it

Area of Learning: PSED   **Focus: Sense of Community**

Name: ....

Individual target: Talk about or indicate what I like and don't like   **Key person:** ....

Try a tasting and smelling game, talking about what ☺ likes and does not like. Use this as a springboard to talk about and compare favourite foods and treats, sharing your thoughts with each other.

Use Velcro to mount photographs of activities onto a felt board. Invite ☺ to choose what to do that session. Use the board to build a visual timetable. Revisit it to talk about how the session went. What did ☺ enjoy?

Make a photograph album of your activities in the setting. Share this with ☺, talking about what ☺ likes and dislikes about the group.

When ☺ expresses strong feelings, draw ☺ to a peaceful place to calm down. Help ☺ talk about his/her feelings. What happened? What didn't you like? What would you like to do instead? How can we sort it out?

Offer ☺ simple concrete choices between activities and resources. Allow ☺ to make a choice from a selection by looking, reaching or vocalising. For older children, add your own commentary: 'You look as if you are enjoying that because...'

Use a plan/do/review structure – the key person helps ☺ to think about what ☺ wants to do and how it is going, and then to talk about the session and express feelings about how it went.

Use a feelings board. Help ☺ mount pictures or photographs of things that ☺ likes and dislikes at the group under a big smiley or sad face labels.

During Circle Time, use a sentence completion game such as 'I went to nursery and I liked...' or 'I didn't like it when...'

Self-confidence and Self-esteem

Many children who have BESD also have issues of low self-esteem and self-confidence. Here are some ideas of how to support them, and keep yourself feeling positive too.

▲●■ Links to Area of Learning

We know that children thrive when their emotional needs are being met and also that they fail to thrive if consistent care and emotional support is absent. Earlier in the book we saw how certain patterns of early care, inconsistency and attachment difficulty can lead to emotional and behavioural difficulties. The main area of difficulty for these children is likely to be low self-esteem and low confidence. We learn confidence through trying things out and meeting with success – the more we succeed, the more we are motivated to have another go. For children who meet failure or rebuttal, the opposite can be true. Your role is to provide experiences and activities in which the children can feel successful and thereby feel positive about themselves and more willing to learn.

There are three main approaches to raising a child's self-esteem and self-confidence. The three approaches can be used in parallel. The first approach is to provide a level of security that helps a child to develop confidence and to explore. This can be done by making sure that there is a consistent and dependable key person with whom the child with BESD can form a positive and enduring relationship. This person provides an 'emotional anchor' for the child and may disapprove of certain behaviours, but always makes it clear that the child is valued and accepted for who they are. The second approach is to make sure that the expectations on the child are appropriate and that there are regular opportunities for meeting success and receiving positive praise. This might involve making sure that you do not expect too great a change at once when intervening to encourage appropriate behaviour. It also means making sure that the learning outcome is suitable for the child, given the various difficulties that the child has. Thirdly, there needs to be positive behaviour management. This means setting clear boundaries, finding a way of containing the child's strong feelings and reactions, and managing incidents firmly, assertively and calmly.

Of course, this is all easy to say. When it comes down to it, you also need to ensure that the needs of the other children are not compromised and that everyone stays safe and can make free choices in their play. This is quite a hard balancing act and you will need to lean on your colleagues and support staff in order to preserve your own self-esteem and confidence.

Your aim for all the children is to help them to respond to significant experiences, showing a range of feelings when appropriate. You also need to help them to develop awareness of their own needs, views and feelings, and be sensitive to the needs, views and feelings of others. Finally, you need to help the children develop respect for their own cultures and beliefs and those of other people.

> Make sure that the expectations on the child are appropriate and that there are regular opportunities for meeting success and receiving positive praise.

Achievement Chart

Name.............................

▲●■ Assessment records

You will find an assessment record for working out which skills and competencies the child has already acquired on the next two pages. As a starting point, look out for and work on behaviours that are sometimes but not yet always demonstrated.

Assessment sheet: Self-confidence and Self-esteem

Name: .... Key person: ....

Personal, Social and Emotional Development   Emotional Development: Self-confidence and Self-esteem

Development matters	What I do now	Never	Sometimes	Always
			Enter date observed	
Finding comfort	Have a favourite toy or plaything for security*			
	Show care and concern for others			
	Show attachment to one favourite adult			
	Can be comforted and calmed by certain adults			
	Am comforted by a favourite activity/music			
Demonstrating feelings	My key person knows from my behaviour how I'm feeling*			
	Indicate to you whether I am happy or sad			
	Recognise happy, sad and angry expressions in others			
	Use one or two feelings words independently			
Making choices	Choose between different playthings			
	Choose between different playmates*			
	Indicate what I want without upsetting others			
	Assert myself appropriately			
	Offer a toy when asked for it			
	Pass a toy without throwing it			
	Ask for a toy without snatching			
	Opt in for activities at group time			
	Use the phrases 'I want...' or 'I like...'			

Recognising danger

- Say 'no' when others try to lead me on*
- Stay within the confines of the setting
- Follow simple safety rules
- Hold a hand when walking during outings
- Walk sensibly when indoors
- Climb down from heights safely

Self-confidence

- Show pleasure in some of the playthings
- Show pleasure in some of the activities
- Confident to respond to an adult one-to-one
- Confident to participate in free play
- Confident to handle changes in routine
- Confident around new adults*

Self-esteem

- Look content and settled 50% of the session
- Manage not to upset others 50% of the session
- Demonstrate some friendly behaviour*
- Talk about myself positively
- Will allow myself to be corrected

Early Learning Goals:

Respond to significant experiences, showing a range of feelings when appropriate.
Have a developing awareness of their own needs, views and feelings, and are sensitive to the needs, views and feelings of others.
Have a developing respect for their own cultures and beliefs and those of other people.

▲ ● ■ Look, listen and note

These are some particular things to observe and note for children who have BESD or, indeed, if you are worried about any child's low self-esteem and self-confidence.

• Observe how confident the baby or toddler is to play all by itself when adults are close by to watch. What happens when the adult moves away?

• How has confidence changed since the child has settled in? Does confidence still depend on the key person being close by? Will the child respond positively to other adults yet?

• Observe, note and then share information about how the child responds when happy, excited, angry, frustrated, anxious or upset.

• Provide opportunities for talking about home and life outside of the setting. Observe how ready the child is to talk, and the feelings he or she expresses.

• Observe if and how the child uses imaginative play to act out experiences and to discharge feelings.

• How does the child respond to success and praise? Note any incidences where the child damages his or her own creations or attempts to destroy other people's achievements or possessions.

• Observe and record any incidences of attempted bullying or being bullied.

▲ ● ■ Effective practice

• The appointment of an emotionally strong key person is crucial. Take care to match the worker to the child's needs and personality – if there is a 'clash' of temperaments, this will not work.

• Try to establish a shared understanding between parents or carers and professionals within the setting as to how to interpret the child's behaviour and feelings and how to manage them.

• Try to find things to praise the child for each session, and commend any successes publicly so that other children see positives too.

• Always listen to both sides of a dispute and, where feasible, make suggestions that enable children to work out their own solutions.

• Adopt the same rules for everyone so that each child can see that boundaries are fair and consistently applied. Stay calm (in your outside appearance) so that the child with BESD sees you as standing firm on the behaviour but not rejecting them emotionally as a person.

• Make an achievement chart (there is a photocopiable example on page 93) so that the child with BESD can see positive improvement and change in learning or behaviour.

• Make a 'feelings box'. If something has really upset the child, write it down for them and post it into the box. Later, fetch it out to talk about together.

▲ ● ■ How to use the play plans

On pages 59 to 64 you will find six photocopiable play plans for those skills marked with an asterisk on the assessment sheets on pages 56 and 57. Each play plan contains eight interventions that you could try. There are two blank spaces to add your own personalised interventions oto each play plan.

Play plan: The magic of cuddlies

Name: ....   Key person: ....

Area of Learning: PSED   Focus: Self-confidence and Self-esteem   Individual target: Have a favourite toy or plaything for security

Watch out for times when ☺ takes out frustrations on the cuddly toy – this may be a sign that things are not going well. Step up your support and use the nurture corner (page 21) before difficult incidents take place.

At rest times, tuck the cuddly in beside ☺ and attach it safely to the cot if you can so that it does not become lost.

When ☺ is feeling upset or angry, draw ☺ to one side and talk softly. As ☺ gets older, you will be able to have ☺ tell the cuddly toy all about it.

When ☺ is older, use the cuddly toy in your role play, acting out ways of behaving so that ☺ can make suggestions and tell the cuddly what to do.

Vulnerable babies and toddlers can derive great comfort from cuddlies, though sometimes need help to do this. Let ☺ choose a cuddly toy and keep it exclusively for ☺. Bring it out for cuddling whenever ☺ is stressed or unhappy.

If ☺ throws the cuddly away in anger, talk about how ☺ is feeling, pick the cuddly up gently and place it nearby to keep an eye on it. Don't criticise ☺ for 'hurting' it.

Try to keep a balance between keeping the cuddly hygienic and not destroying its smell and consistency – smell is an important source of reassurance and comfort to babies. The same is true for blankets that some children use as comforters.

As you sing and nurse ☺, introduce the cuddly as well and sing to it; you are beginning to give the cuddly a 'persona' that, in time, ☺ might find comforting.

Dip in

Play plan: Reading the signs

Name: .... **Key person:** ....

Area of Learning: PSED **Focus:** Self-confidence and Self-esteem **Individual target:** My key person knows from my behaviour how I'm feeling

When you see ☺ behaving in typical ways, give ☺ some simple feelings words and encourage ☺ to talk about the feelings behind the behaviour.

Share the photographs you have gathered with ☺ and use these as a springboard for talking about feelings and behaviours.

As a key person, spend time observing ☺ in different moods and on different occasions, spotting the repertoire of behaviour that ☺ shows. Analyse your observations to help you understand ☺. (This is relevant to all ages including babies.)

Make sure that visiting staff and supply teachers have sight of the communication book before they start work with you.

Use simple words to interpret ☺'s behaviour to other children – '☺ is still learning how to share. When she snatches toys from you, it is her way of saying she wants to play with it. Tell me if you need help.'

Create a communication book to share with colleagues. For example, 'When ☺ is feeling bored, he might throw the equipment and look for your reaction. This might be because ☺ needs your help to initiate his own play. Try moving in beside ☺ to extend the play and make suggestions.'

If ☺ seems unsettled, withdraw to a quiet area and try to settle ☺ before any difficulties arise. Sometimes you can prevent outbursts simply by 'reading' ☺'s behaviour early on.

With the necessary consents, collect digital photographs of ☺ in all sorts of moods, behaviours and 'colours' – gather positives as well as negativeimages.

Dip in

Play plan: Dial-a-friend

Name: ....

Key person: ....

Focus: Self-confidence and Self-esteem

Individual target: Choose between different playmates

Area of Learning: PSED

Ask ☺ who ☺ would like to play with that session and what ☺ would like to do. Go together to ask that child; ☺ asks if you would play football later?' Offer to be there if necessary. Keep it short and successful.

From time to time, collect information from all the children about whom they would like to play with [this is a simple form of 'sociometry']. If children begin to name ☺ as a playmate, then you have been successful in your target.

When ☺ is still settling in, plan a high level of individual attention and small group work.

Children at this stage define friends as anyone they play with at the time, so use the friendship board to try to set up a range of different partnerships and activities.

State your friendship rules clearly before any play activity, using role play and small world play to rehearse these. Practise the rules on a separate occasion.

Make a friendship board with each child's photograph on. Talk to ☺ about this, reminding ☺ of what they played with when ☺ spent time with each child.

Use Circle Time to reinforce learning each other's names. Plan activities that involve getting to know one another. Plan 'mini Circle Times' with a high level of support for ☺ if big groups present difficulties.

Rotate the children involved in small group activities so that ☺ plays with everyone, under your supervision and with your support. Plan different activities depending on the children involved, so that ☺ tastes many different ways of playing and relating. Keep the activities short and successful.

Dip in

Play plan: OK to say NO

Name: ....

Key person: ....

Area of Learning: PSED   Focus: Self-confidence and Self-esteem   Individual target: Say 'no' when others try to lead me on

If ☺ is older, challenge ☺ to find one time that session when someone wanted ☺ to be naughty and ☺ managed to say, 'no'. Ask ☺ to come and tell you about it. Praise warmly.

Always talk about difficult incidents later and make it clear to ☺ that there is usually a choice in how to behave. Role play the other ways so that ☺ can practise more appropriate ways of behaving.

When you talk together about incidents of behaviour that have gone badly wrong, talk about how ☺ might have behaved differently. What stops that happening? Talk about how to say 'no' the next time that someone tries to get ☺ into trouble.

Use small world play to act out a situation in which a certain character always tries to get ☺ into trouble. Practise saying 'No!'

Play this version of 'Simon says': if Simon tells the children to do something appropriate (such as smile at a friend) then they should do it. If he tells them to do something inappropriate (such as stamp and shout), then they should just say, 'No!'.

Make up photographs or story cards about children doing different things. Post appropriate behaviours into a smiley box and inappropriate behaviours into the sad box.

Use two puppets (one behaving well, one badly) to act out scenarios. Encourage ☺ to take turns in handling each puppet (give each puppet a name and different characteristics). Discuss the right way to behave and how it feels when others behave differently.

Use observation to identify triggers to ☺'s difficult behaviour. If this involves certain combinations of children, plan alternative activities and grouping for a while to break the cycle.

Play plan: Pleased to meet you

Name: ....

Key person: ....

Area of Learning: PSED   Focus: Self-confidence and Self-esteem

Individual target: Confident around new adults.

Use a communication book to help any new teacher or practitioner prepare for tuning into ☺'s behaviour. Back this up with clear information about rules and boundaries that have been put in place so that you aim for consistency in management.

Plan for transitions especially carefully, if possible with a visit or two and a familiar adult to bridge the transition period.

Warn any new professional or visitor that ☺ might be unsettled at first because there is someone new. Suggest that they ignore silliness for the first few minutes (if it is safe to do so) until ☺ has settled down.

Always give ☺ plenty of notice when there is going to be a new adult in charge. If possible, show a photograph or arrange for ☺ to meet that person during a visit.

Work with ☺ to collect a portfolio of good news (about happy play sessions and proud achievements) that can be shared with any newcomer. In this way, you will balance 'bad news' with good.

If a new key person is to be allocated for a baby, make sure whenever possible there is a lead-in time when both the familiar and the new adult are both present.

Make a list of activities that have been particularly successful for ☺ so that these can be dipped into until ☺ is used to the new adults.

Make a personal picture book about 'my new school' and use this for ☺ to talk through ahead of starting school. This will help ☺ to feel more secure about what is going to happen there.

Dip in

Play plan: Making friends

Name: .... Key person: ....

Area of Learning: PSED Focus: Self-confidence and Self-esteem Individual target: Demonstrate some friendly behaviour

Take photographs of ☺ 'being friendly' and talk about these together afterwards. What was ☺ doing that helped the other child know that ☺ was being a friend?

If other children have been put off playing with ☺, help ☺ reflect on what ☺ could do differently next time. Set up a fail-proof short play session (using your full support and supervision) to demonstrate to ☺ that it does work!

Play simple turn-taking games to introduce ☺ to: why games have rules; how to give and receive instructions; ways of finding out who goes first; working out what to do when it's not your turn; giving positive feedback to each other; and coping with losing.

Use puppets and role play for ☺ to demonstrate and ask each other to play, how to negotiate what to play, how to compromise and how to work together so that each person has fun. Follow this up by reminding ☺ in real situations.

Model friendly meetings and greetings with babies – as if they are saying hello to each other!

Draw some simple signs to represent basic friendship rules – for example: ask don't snatch; smiley face; wait your turn; listen to each other; be kind. Point to them to celebrate and praise good friendship behaviour or to remind ☺ of the rules.

Help ☺ make up a game to play and then support ☺ while ☺ invites another child to try it out. Praise all signs of friendly behaviour specifically – 'Well done for giving Joe a turn too!'

Give ☺ a special responsibility to 'be a friend' to a puppet or another child for one session. Stay close to support.

Behaviour and Self-control

It is through their behaviour and poor self-control that children who have BESD demonstrate their most obvious needs. Here are some activity ideas for supporting them inclusively.

▲ ● ■ Links to Area of Learning

Children learn how to behave through the boundaries we set them and through the emotional support and encouragement we provide to help them. They learn to understand what is right and wrong and why. They also learn to consider the consequences of their words and actions for themselves and others. Again, it becomes easy to see how this process can go wrong. You may have children within your setting who have not learned what a boundary, a rule or a code of behaviour is. They may have learned to behave in any way that they feel like until an adult steps in to stop them – it does not occur to them that they have a choice in how to behave or that they can control their own behaviour. Other children may have learned to behave inappropriately because it secures for them the level of attention and predictability that they seem to crave. Others too will react very emotionally to situations when they feel thwarted or when things go wrong – because they have grown up with very 'prickly' and reactive temperaments probably linked to low self-esteem. It is difficult to tease apart where a child's behaviour might have stemmed from but it will be occurring to you by now that the picture is far more complex than a child who is simply 'naughty' or 'cannot behave'.

The way forward is clear. You need to provide a calm, caring environment that provides clear and consistent boundaries and is, at the end of the day, an encouraging and supportive place in which to develop and to change. There may come a point when you decide that a child's BESD are so great as to constitute special educational needs, since the approaches you use have to be significantly additional and different to usual. You can read about this in the Series handbook, *The Inclusive Practice Handbook* (Scholastic). Most local authority support services will give you general advice as part of your Early Years Action, especially if a child's behaviour is severely disruptive to others. If specific advice is necessary, you may need to monitor a child's needs as Early Years Action Plus with assessment and support from an outside professional. Some families are referred by their GP to a Child and Adolescent Mental Health Service (CAMHS) team in order to work more therapeutically with a child's BESD, or there might be a social worker or family support worker involved if there are family issues. In other words, if a behaviour problem is severe you should not be alone.

▲ ● ■ Assessment records

You will find an assessment record for working out which skills and competencies the child has already acquired on the next two pages. As a starting point, look out for and work on behaviours that are sometimes but not yet always demonstrated.

> You need to provide a calm, caring environment that provides clear and consistent boundaries and is an encouraging and supportive place in which to develop and to change.

Assessment sheet: Behaviour and Self-control

Name: .... Key person: ....

Personal, Social and Emotional Development

Emotional Development: Behaviour and Self-control

Development matters	What I do now	Never	Sometimes	Always
			Enter date observed	
Accepts praise	Soothed by a warm response from an adult			
	Join in with a celebratory clap and cheer			
	Do something to gain a concrete reward*			
	Repeat an activity that was praised before			
	Stop being silly when I am ignored			
Simple boundaries	Respond to a simple boundary*			
	Anticipate the routines of the group			
	Join Circle Time for five minutes			
	Join story time for five minutes			
	Join the whole of group time			
	Aware of the boundaries and expectations of the group*			
Compliance	Turn when my name is called			
	Stop momentarily when told 'no'			
	Comply with a simple request			
Simple rules	Follow a rule with support			
	Contribute to making up a simple set of rules*			
	Tell you what the rules are			
	Follow the rules of the group 75% of the time			

Other people's needs					
Aware of what is mine and what belongs to others*					
Aware when other children are hurt					
Show care and concern if other children are upset					
Can explain why I shouldn't run/hit/kick/throw					
Can accept the need to take turns and to share*					

Standing up for myself					
Resist other children who try to snatch from me					
Call for help if others try to hurt me					
Use words not actions to indicate what I want					
Organise a simple turn-taking or team game for others					
Help to look after new starters					

Early Learning Goals:

Understand what is right and wrong and why.
Consider the consequences of their words and actions for themselves and others.

▲ ● ■ Look, listen and note

You may decide to monitor a child's challenging behaviour using a diary or S.T.A.R. observation (see page 15). However, a curricular approach is also helpful so that you can see how the child is progressing through the EYFS. Here are some particular things to look out for with a child who has BESD.

• How does the child respond when other children are hurt or upset? Is there any attempt to comfort or to make things better?

• Does the child understand that 'no' means 'no'?

• Is the child able to receive and follow through a simple instruction? (You cannot expect them to comply with your request if they have not received it or understood it.)

• Are there any signs that a child would like to please you? Does the child enjoy praise? If so, who from and what kind of praise? Do other rewards work better perhaps?

• Can the child contribute to making up a set of simple rules for the group? Is there any understanding yet of why these rules are necessary?

• Is there any understanding yet that certain behaviour (such as hurting others) is wrong? Can the child understand the concepts of 'being kind' or 'being a friend'?

▲ ● ■ Effective practice

Always pair any concrete reward (playing with a certain toy or a treat) with social praise so that, in time, the child will find the praise rewarding in itself.

• State rules clearly and simply, and give warning before intervening with a sanction. For example – 'Be kind, Jack…' and then, if the child does not comply, 'You are going inside because you tried to hurt Sophie.'

• However you feel inside, appear as calm and neutral as you can. If you add your own anger or frustration to the child's, you will only 'fan the flames' of a tantrum.

• Do not feel that you have to confront every single piece of difficult behaviour. Make a stand on rules that really matter and use humour and distraction to avoid other potential clashes.

• Try to deal with difficult behaviour by withdrawing the child from the audience whenever possible.

• Share your approaches with colleagues so that you provide emotional support to each other at what might be a very difficult time for you.

• Keep parents and carers in touch with your interventions.

• You will find all the suggestions in the 'Removing the barriers' chapter (starting on page 17) very relevant to managing children's behaviour and self-control.

▲ ● ■ How to use the play plans

On pages 69 to 74 you will find six photocopiable play plans for those skills marked with an asterisk on the assessment sheets on pages 66 and 67. Each play plan contains eight interventions that you could try. There are two blank spaces to add your own personalised interventions to each play plan.

Sequential

Play plan: Well done!

Area of Learning: PSED   **Focus:** Behaviour and Self-control

Name: ....   **Key person:** ....

Individual target: Do something to gain a concrete reward

1 Vulnerable children may not understand the concepts of reward and praise. Try this simple reward and compliance training using a small eatable treat. Say the baby or toddler's name and, as ☺ turns to you, pop the treat in ☺'s mouth and praise warmly. Repeat during the session.

2 Progress to giving a simple instruction – for example '☺, put the brick in the box, please' – reward with a treat and warm praise. Repeat four or five times in order to teach the sequence: pay attention, receive instruction, do, receive praise.

3 Arrange for two or three short periods of structured teaching each session (as before). Sit down away from distractions and use very simple play tasks to reinforce compliance. Start to reserve the eatable treat for the end of the teaching period.

4 Switch eatable treats for stickers or stamps. Still use your warm praise and continue with the short spells of structured teaching as you gradually build up attention and compliance.

5 Try 'when' statements – 'When you have tidied up, it will be time to play outside.' Make one enjoyable activity contingent upon another less enjoyable one.

6 Use the 'How am I doing?' progress sheet on page 93 as a concrete record that ☺ has tried hard to 'do as you are nicely asked'.

7 State one of your group rules clearly and explain that you will be on the look out for ☺ doing just that. Make sure you catch ☺ following the rule (with support if necessary) and reward with a sticker and praise.

8 Use the reward sticker chart on page 89 to set an individual target for ☺ and record progress as ☺ gathers stickers. Work out a good reward for the completed chart and use your enthusiasm to keep up the interest.

Dip in

Play plan: Staying put

Name: .... Key person: ....

Area of Learning: PSED Focus: Behaviour and Self-control Individual target: Respond to a simple boundary

Use colour coding to distinguish noisy play areas from quiet restful areas. For example, create a nurture corner in blues and purples with soft coverings and matching cushions.

If you are spending time in a large hall, cover up potential distractions with sheets or screens. Use distraction and tight planning to ensure that there is no time left to 'push the boundaries'.

Play physical games such as running and dodging in order to encourage ☺ and the other children to 'find their own space' and not touch each other as they move safely at speed.

Follow consistent routines when you go outside to play, using visual boundaries to show children where they may and may not go.

Provide a special place for ☺ to withdraw to when ☺ is showing signs of unsettled behaviour. Ideas include having a special cardboard box house with a few calming toys inside. Other children should leave ☺ alone until invited in.

If kicking others is a problem, encourage everyone to wear slippers inside. Find an appropriate activity for ☺ to do with hands during group time, so that they are gainfully occupied.

Allow ☺ to sit on a cushion or chair at group time if fidgeting is a problem. Mark a circle on the ground or place carpet squares in a ring to encourage sitting nicely in a circle.

Use safety locks and catches on kitchen doors and accessible cupboards rather than constantly reminding ☺ not to enter.

Dip in

Play plan: Doing it our way

Name: ....   Key person: ....

Area of Learning: PSED   Focus: Behaviour and Self-control   Individual target: Aware of the boundaries and expectations of the group

Even with babies and toddlers, be on the look out for acceptable behaviour and use targeted praise to show that you have noticed it: 'Well done ☺ – you're sitting down ready for your tea!'

Make sure that you teach ☺ what the behaviour words you use actually mean in practice – in other words, practise being gentle, quiet, sitting still, being kind and so on.

Regular routines for babies are a vital part of helping them to develop an awareness of what is expected of them in the group.

When a situation has gone badly wrong, go to a quiet place and talk about it calmly. Shut your eyes and visualise together 'what it would look like' if ☺ could re-run the 'film' and start again.

Give the impression of real confidence that you expect ☺ to follow your requests – even if this is unlikely. Your confidence might well rub off on ☺!

Encourage ☺ to help you show a new starter around the setting, telling them all about the things that you do and where you are allowed to play.

Encourage ☺ to explain to a puppet or soft toy all about the daily routines of the group, showing the puppet where the children may and may not play, explaining why.

Practise positive affirmations to convince ☺ that ☺ can fulfil the expectations in the group setting. For example: 'I can play with the cars without hurting'; 'I can be a friend'; or 'I can line up and come in the room quietly!'

Dip in

Play plan: Going by the rule

Name: ....   Key person: ....

Area of Learning: PSED   Focus: Behaviour and Self-control   Individual target: Contribute to making up a simple set of rules

Make simple symbols or signs (along the lines of road signs, perhaps) to represent simple rules and display these on the wall. Point to them if you need to remind ☺ or another child to remember the rule.

Spend some time talking to ☺ about why ☺ felt that this rule was a good rule to have. Help ☺ to think about the other children's points of view. Help ☺ to also see that the rule will help ☺ in some way.

Use the story on page 00 to initiate a discussion about rules. What rules would you suggest for the puppies? Why do we need rules? For younger children, choose one rule and act it out with soft toys 'stroke gently, don't scratch'.

Notice when individual children are following rules and use group time to commend them, telling the other children what you noticed them doing. Make sure that ☺ is included in this, even if you prompted or supported the positive behaviour at the time.

At each group time, remind the children of your group rules. Repeat them to ☺ before transition times or times of day when ☺ is most likely to show difficult behaviour.

Act out a simple scenario with soft toys and see if ☺ can spot when the toys break the rules. Ask ☺ to tell them what to do instead.

Teach a very simple board game to ☺ using simple rules. Show that rules tell us what to do and also keep it fair for everyone.

Use group time to talk together about rules within the group. Decide on three or four very simple rules that everyone agrees would be helpful.

Dip in

Play plan: Mine and yours

Name: .... **Key person:** ....

Area of Learning: PSED **Focus: Behaviour and Self-control** **Individual target: Aware of what is mine and what belongs to others**

Hold a regular 'show and tell' session at group time in which all the children can bring in something special from home and share it. Have a special place to keep the items safe for the rest of the session.

Teach ☺ how to ask for resources from another child without snatching. Encourage ☺ to pass resources when asked. Notice and praise this behaviour at other times during the session.

Make up a game in which one puppet wants to play with its own toys at the group but the other puppet doesn't understand that it can't play with them too. Talk about shared toys and your own toys.

Encourage ☺ to empty pockets before going home (if this is a problem) so that the group's toys can live in their special places. Deal with this in a matter of fact and practical way.

Have a special box for ☺ to place any toys and possessions from home. Place this in sight, but out of reach (especially if there are toy weapons brought in from home).

When using exciting collage pieces, invite each child to take turns to choose a few of the 'best bits' to place in their own pots before starting work.

Try to keep each baby's clothing and toys individual to them (rather than 'pooled' clothing to change into) so that they begin to develop a sense of personal possession.

Find time to talk about things that go home with you (paintings, models, drawings) and things that stay in the group (the play dough, small toys, crayons) – when you think about it, it can be very confusing!

Dip in

Play plan: Sharing and caring

Name: .... Key person: ....

Area of Learning: PSED Focus: Behaviour and Self-control Individual target: Can accept the need to take turns and to share

Try to arrange for ☺ to have a birthday cake or dish of treats to share out with the other children and ask ☺ to help you work out how to pass it round fairly.

Make a game of challenging ☺ to actually lose at something. At first, this is easiest if the competitor is a puppet who, you explain, has never won anything before.

Play with puppets or soft toys, with ☺ showing them how to take turns or to share. Make things go wrong occasionally so that ☺ has to 'police' the game and explain what to do to the puppets.

Use observable indicators of time passing, such as sand timers or cooking timers, to signal turns on the computer or playing with a toy car. Encourage ☺ to set these going and to signal the next turn.

Choose play activities that are more fun to play when there are two of you – kicking a ball to each other or blowing bubbles for another child to pop. This makes turn taking natural and enjoyable.

Play with the train or race track together. Set up a game where it is first the red engine/car's turn, and then the blue engine/car's turn to win the race or make a circuit of the track.

Keep shared activities (such as using the slide) to a very small group when ☺ is there so that ☺ does not have long to wait at first.

Use a 'Speaking Ted' at Circle Time – whoever is holding Ted gets to speak or to have a turn. All the others must watch or listen.

■SCHOLASTIC
www.scholastic.co.uk

Language for Thinking

If you can support children with BESD towards developing the language for thinking, then they have a better chance of reflecting about their own behaviour and thinking ahead before acting impulsively.

▲ ● ■ Links to Area of Learning

> You need to acknowledge and contain the strong feelings that often underlie their challenging behaviour, but also help the children to handle these by using calming techniques and by talking.

Practitioners who work with children who have BESD often comment on the children's difficulties in listening or processing language – as if some of these children react emotionally to the moment and do not have the words or thoughts to reflect, reason or be reasoned with. That is why it has been chosen to include this focus of learning.

In the early stages of acquiring language for thinking, young children start to understand what is said to them by familiar people in familiar contexts. When thinking clearly, they are able to respond to simple requests and begin to use language as a powerful means of widening contacts, sharing feelings, experiences and thoughts. For children who are highly emotional (for whatever reason), this process is much harder. It is difficult to think clearly when the emotional, more primitive, area of your brain is taking control and causing you to react before you think.

Working with children who have BESD is a balancing act. You need to acknowledge and contain the strong feelings that often underlie their challenging behaviour, but also help the children to handle these by using calming techniques and by talking. Through talking and reasoning, we are all helped to make sense of and to release bottled up feelings, enabling us to think more clearly. 'Logical brain' begins to take over from 'emotional brain' and this is all part of developing emotional literacy. We can also use our talking and thinking to explore other ways of behaving and to accept reasoning and explanation from others. We can be helped to wait for things, rather than have our gratification met immediately. We learn that we can influence the world by ways other than shouting and lashing out. We begin to think and talk about other people's points of view apart from our own.

In time, most children will begin to use talk instead of action to rehearse, reorder and reflect on past experience, linking significant events from their own experience and from stories, paying attention to sequence and how events lead into one another. They begin to see patterns in their experiences through linking cause and effect, sequencing, ordering and grouping. They also begin to use talk to develop imaginary situations and this is the stage at which small world play, role play and the use of stories and rhymes can be used very effectively with children who have BESD in order to explore alternative ways of behaving and reacting. Your support should enable them to achieve the Early Learning Goals of using language to imagine and recreate roles and experiences and using talk to organise, sequence and clarify thinking, ideas, feelings and events.

▲ ● ■ Assessment records

You will find an assessment record for working out which skills and competencies the child has already acquired on the next two pages. As a starting point, look out for and work on behaviours that are sometimes but not yet always demonstrated.

Assessment sheet: Language for Thinking

Name: ....   Key person: ....

Communication, Language and Literacy

Language for Communication and Thinking: Language for Thinking

Enter date observed

Development matters	What I do now	Never	Sometimes	Always
Sending out messages	Stop shouting or crying when an adult approaches			
	Call out to an adult			
	Use appropriate actions to attract your attention			
Receiving messages	Look at you briefly when you talk to me			
	Cooperate with simple care routines*			
	Follow through a simple direction			
	Do as I am nicely asked 50% of the time			
First words	Use words to attract your attention			
	Say 'yes' and 'no'*			
	Tell you what's wrong			
	Use some simple feelings words			
	Link actions with words			
	Follow a simple gesture or sign (such as a sign for 'no')			
	Join in a simple two-way action game*			
	Make a puppet happy/sad/angry			
Talk about my behaviour	Talk about new ways of behaving*			
	Have language to explain			
	Link cause with effect ('because he pushed me')			

Talk about my feelings

Understand that feelings can affect how we behave

Understand that other people have feelings too

Understand that group rules apply to me

Imagining alternatives

Talk about what I might have done instead

Use puppets and small world play to think about behaviour*

Talk about future events and imagine how to behave appropriately

Use talk to describe imaginary situations and how to behave in them

Learning from experience

Remember what worked well last time and do it again

Know when to ask an adult for help when dealing with others

Feel positive about my own progress*

Early Learning Goals:

Use language to imagine and recreate roles and experiences.
Use talk to organise, sequence and clarify thinking, ideas, feelings and events.

▲ ● ■ Look, listen and note

You will need to observe and monitor all the children's progress through the EYFS. Here are some things to watch out for especially when working with children who have BESD.

• Observe what methods the child uses to convey messages about what they want, what they need and what they feel. Does it feel as though they are communicating these messages at you or to you?

• Note down how the child responds to the adults and children around her/him, and keep a record of both positive circumstances and negative circumstances. What seems to trigger a positive response and what seems to trigger a negative one? If you cannot spot a pattern yet, keep observing.

• As the child develops, look out for the first evidence that the child is using language and thought, rather than action and emotional reaction, when faced with a challenging situation. This is a real turning point.

• Note occasions when the child appeared able to accept your reasoning and explanation. This is most likely to happen when the child is calm, rather than when emotional and in the midst of an upset; accepting reason comes a long time before being able to see it through into practice.

▲ ● ■ Effective practice

• Even if a child is showing an emotional reaction rather than using language, add your own words as a commentary to what is going on: 'Stop that now. You are feeling very cross. Come here, settle yourself down and then we'll sort it out together.'

• Use puppets and role play to act out likely scenarios before they happen. This will help the child to think about how to behave. Also, use them to re-enact situations that went especially well or badly, and to reflect on them together.

• Make sure that there is a regular opportunity for the child to talk to their key person about what they have been doing and what they are feeling.

• Use the key person's detailed knowledge of a child to help that child remember past events, what happened and why. This will help the child to begin to make connections with past behaviours and feelings.

• Use explanation and talk to help the child link 'cause and effect' as they relate to behaviour and reactions.

• Use stories to reflect on behaviour and remind the child of them from time to time if they seem relevant to the situation in hand. Humour is a brilliant tool to use if appropriate to the situation.

• Develop narratives that externalise the behaviour from the child – 'Tell your hands that it is listening time now, so they need to stay on your lap'.

▲ ● ■ How to use the play plans

On pages 79 to 84 you will find six photocopiable play plans for those skills marked with an asterisk on the assessment sheets on pages 76 and 77. Each play plan contains eight interventions that you could try. There are two blank spaces to add your own personalised interventions to each play plan.

Sequential

Play plan: Helping out

Name: .... **Key person:** ....

Area of Learning: CLL   **Focus: Language for Thinking**

Individual target: Cooperate with simple care routines

1 Unsettled babies may be difficult to care for because they arch their backs and scream. Use strong distraction techniques to catch their interest – a bright mobile above the changing mat, a funny song at changing time or gentle talking at feeding time.

2 Give ☺ little responsibilities to carry out with your support.

3 Give ☺ little responsibilities to carry out with your support.

4 Work out the steps needed for ☺ to, for example, pull trousers up or down. Use gentle words and prompts to encourage ☺ to do the first step independently and then help for the rest of the procedure.

5 Have set routines for things such as going to the toilet: 'Close door – toilet – toilet paper – wash hands – taps off'. Mount pictures in sequence to remind ☺ how to carry out a self-care activity. Celebrate all signs of independence.

6 With little ones, always 'negotiate' a care activity before carrying it out to give them warning! For example, approach from the front, show the cloth and say what you are going to do before wiping a child's face – never just materialise from behind!

7 Rather than nag ☺ about what to do (such as putting on a coat to go outside), pause to ask: 'We're going outside. What do we need to do first?' Praise ☺ for remembering. Try to stick to the same routines.

8 Warn ☺ before the next stage in your session routine so that ☺ can start thinking about what to do next. For example – 'When you hear the music, it will be time to tidy up'.

Sequential

Play plan: Yes and no

Name: .... Key person: ....

Area of Learning: CLL   Focus: Language for Thinking   Individual target: Say 'yes' and 'no'

1 If ☺ is still very young, signal 'yes' (thumbs up) or 'no' (a flat hand facing down, moved across your body from left to right). Use ☺'s name to establish eye contact first and speak the word at the same time.

2 If ☺ is reluctant to say 'yes', choose something that ☺ really likes to play with. Hold it up and ask, 'Do you want the engine?', emphasising the key word. Prompt 'yes' and then pass it over. Repeat as required.

3 Offer ☺ a choice between two actual objects. Hold up two toys/ items/snack foods, one after the other, and say, 'Do you want this one or this one?' When ☺ reaches or points, say, 'Yes – ☺ wants the ...!'

4 Use a series of photographs of your activities. Sit down with ☺ and show each one. Ask, 'Do you want to play with the ... today?' Encourage a yes/ no response.

5 Use register time to encourage ☺ to make a 'yes' response. At first, just establish eye contact at ☺'s name. Later, expect a wave or a hand up. Later still, pause for a 'yes'. Praise all compliance warmly.

6 Make two post boxes, one for 'yes' and one for 'no'. Look at 'feelings' photographs in a small group with ☺. Discuss the photos and ask: 'Do you feel happy? Grumpy?' Let them post the pictures in the right box for them.

7 Ask fun group questions that call for a 'YES!' or a 'NO!' response – Are there any elephants in the room today? Does anyone like jelly? Does anyone live in a nest?

8 Begin to teach politeness words to accompany the yes/no response. Teach, model and then reinforce throughout the session the phrases 'yes, please' and 'no thank you'.

Dip in

Play plan: My turn-your turn

Name: .... Key person: ....

Area of Learning: CLL   Focus: Language for Thinking   Individual target: Join in a simple two-way action game

Organise a traffic-light game outside – one child drives around a circuit whilst the other operates a green/amber/red 'light' (with cards). Stay close to support turn-taking and keep the language flowing happily.

At group time, shake a tambourine energetically to attract attention, then beat it once loudly and stop. Encourage the children to shake as you shake and to stop when you stop. Praise ☺ for looking and listening.

'Football' with a partner is a fun activity that helps to burn off energy and keeps a distance between two children as they play. Stay near to ☺ to support as a soft ball is kicked between them, reinforcing the language of turn-taking.

Use mirror play to make silly faces and copy each other. Talk about what you see. Involve another child once ☺ understands the game.

Support ☺ with one other child as they play a blowing and bursting bubbles game. Encourage friendly language and behaviour as you play, such as 'more please' and 'your turn now'.

Set up a 'roll and catch' game with a long tube fixed into position and a ball to roll down it. If ☺ rolls the ball, can another child catch it before it touches the ground? Help ☺ to invite others to play.

Try a regular Music Makers circle time to encourage looking, listening, two-way interaction and linking words to actions. Children respond well to the routine and predictability of this and you can use it to settle behaviour (see Resources, page 96).

You can teach both compliance and linking actions to words by simply encouraging ☺ to join in enjoyable action rhymes. Choose rhymes that either involve ☺ watching your actions and copying, or doing as the rhyme suggests because it's fun to.

Dip in

Play plan: Try and Try

Name: ....

Key person: ....

Area of Learning: CLL

Focus: Language for Thinking

Individual target: Talk about new ways of behaving

When a challenging incident takes place, deal with it at the time and make a note of it. Later, replay the incident with ☺ and seek ideas from ☺ as to how things might go differently next time.

Make sure that ☺ feels that ☺ can begin each session with a fresh start, taking each day at a time.

If something new is about to happen, talk through what it is going to be and invite ☺ to say how ☺ will try to behave in that situation. Consider things that might stop ☺ from behaving well, talking through the potential barriers.

Talk about feelings together. When reviewing a difficult incident, ask 'What might happy ☺ have done?'; 'What might angry ☺ have done?' Use this as a way of talking about ☺'s anger and how you can help ☺ to deal with it.

Catch incidences of successful and sociable play on camera and share them with ☺'s parents and carers. Talk all together about why it went so well.

Point out how other children are behaving and use this to talk about how to be friends or how to avoid hurting others. Always relate this patiently back to ☺, showing that rules are there to help ☺ feel safe and happy too.

Use the photocopiable picture on page 95 as a talking point. What is going on here? What might happen next? What are these children thinking? What could that child do instead?

Even before they are talking, use simple language to talk about other children behaving well: "Look Sam has given that toy to Kiera – kind Sam!"

■SCHOLASTIC
www.scholastic.co.uk

Dip in

Play plan: Puppet pranks

Name: .... Key person: ....

Area of Learning: CLL   Focus: Language for Thinking   Individual target: Use puppets and small world play to think about behaviour

Sometimes it might feel as if you are always having to 'nag' ☺. By using puppets to re-enact what happened, it takes the focus off ☺ yet still allows you to find alternative solutions.

Allow ☺ free reign with small world toys to inform your observations – Is ☺ working cathartically through experiences that are troubling ☺? If you sense this is going on, arrange for ☺ to play alone if ☺ wants to.

Set up small world play around the themes of caring, such as hospitals or schools. Move in to add your commentary and help ☺ focus on helpful deeds and friendly behaviour.

Make your own stick puppets around the theme of 'feelings' using a range of materials, colours and facial expressions. Work in a small group and talk about strong feelings – how they are normal and how you can learn to express them appropriately.

Use puppets to teach useful social skills as well as working through past problems. For example, encourage ☺ to teach a puppet how to ask another child to play, wait a turn or share out the toys.

Arrange for a small world play activity to reflect anything new that is going to happen in ☺'s life, such as a house move or a new baby. Observe closely and help ☺ make sense of it all if necessary.

The magic of puppets is that ☺ can play different roles and begin to understand what incidents feel like from different perspectives. Always make sure that ☺ has the chance to be the 'good' puppet as well as the 'naughty' puppet, and talk to ☺ about feelings as well as behaviours.

Make a reversible glove puppet that shows one side happy and the other angry. Use it to represent feelings as you talk to ☺ about experiences.

Dip in

Play plan: I'm getting there

Name: .... Key person: ....

Area of Learning: CLL   Focus: Language for Thinking   Individual target: Feel positive about my own progress

Use the photocopiable reward sticker chart on page 89 to share a target and celebrate progress towards it.

Always use positive behaviour approaches. Make it clear that it is ☺'s behaviour that is unacceptable rather than ☺ as a person. Praise appropriate behaviour and make sure that you teach a new positive behaviour to replace an inappropriate one.

Use the photocopiable sheet 'How am I doing?' (page 93) with ☺ to share the steps towards a new target or skill.

Share progress with parents and carers and ask them to commend ☺ for any signs of change. They might have received plenty of 'bad news' in the past and it will do the family good to share positive news instead.

When you have a bad day together, try not to convey the message that you are 'back to square one'. Try to remain optimistic, step up your approaches and support and start afresh the next session.

Make sure that you include ☺ in negotiating the next behaviour target. Explain your approach and make it clear what will happen each time ☺ does a certain behaviour and what will happen if ☺ does not.

Keep a photographic record to share with ☺, showing how things have changed positively since ☺ joined the group. Involve ☺ in keeping this up to date.

Ask ☺ at the end of each session what went really well and what ☺ enjoyed doing. Try to hatch a plan together of what ☺ would like to do next session.

Play plan Copy this blank play plan so that you can make your own plan

Area of Learning:

Focus:

Individual target:

Name: ....

Key person: ....

Monitoring sheet Copy this sheet and use it to monitor how your play plans went.

Name: .... Key person: ....

Area of Learning .... Focus ....

Individual target: ....

What we did	How it worked	Next steps

Inclusive Practice in Early Years **Behaviour, emotional and social difficulties**

■SCHOLASTIC
www.scholastic.co.uk

Home plan
Copy this sheet and use it to share your activities at home.

Name: ....   Key person: ....

Area of Learning ....   Focus ....

This week we are helping ....   to ....

It would be really helpful if you could try this at home:

....

How did ....   get on: ....

Summary sheet Copy this sheet and use it as a summary of your work for the next review meeting.

Name: ....

Focus: ....

Individual target ....

Area of Learning ....

Key person: ....

Date: ....

Outcome	Summary of progress	Challenges to be met	Help from home	Next steps

Signed: ....

Date: ....

Inclusive Practice in Early Years **Behaviour, emotional and social difficulties**

Reward sticker chart

My name: ....

Every time I do this

....

I choose a sticker!

When my sticker chart is full, this will happen:

....

S.T.A.R. behaviour chart: bad news

Name: .... **Group:** ....

Use this chart to record six particularly challenging incidences of behaviour. Record the setting (what happened before the incident took place, the context and situation at the time), the trigger (what set off the behaviour), the action (exactly how the child acted) and the response (the result of the child's behaviour and how those around the child responded).

Date	Setting	Trigger	Action	Response

S.T.A.R. behaviour chart: good news

Name: ....   Group: ....

Use this chart to record six particularly impressive (or simply appropriate) incidences of behaviour. Record the setting (what happened before the incident took place, the context and situation at the time), the trigger (what set off the behaviour), the action (exactly how the child acted) and the response (the result of the child's behaviour and how those around the child responded).

Date	Setting	Trigger	Action	Response

Voices

Use this rhyme during Circle Time to practise your different voices. Ask each question and encourage the children to reply using the refrain, changing their voice tones to suit the mood!

Have you got your **squeaky** voices with you all today?

Yes we have, we really have so listen to what we say!

Have you got your **LOUD** voices with you all today?

Yes we have, we really have so listen to what we say!

Have you got your **whiney** voices with you all today?

Yes we have, we really have so listen to what we say!

Have you got your **grumpy** voices with you all today?

Yes we have, we really have so listen to what we say!

Have you got your **quiet** voices with you all today?

Yes we have, we really have so listen to what we say!

Have you got your **happy** voices with you all today?

Yes we have, we really have so listen to what we say!

Hannah Mortimer

Follow up during the session by inviting children to 'try your happy voice'.

How am I doing?

Name of child: ....

Starting date: ....

Write in the targets you are hoping ☺ to achieve, step by step. Encourage ☺ to colour them in or highlight them once each has been successfully achieved. Use the assessment sheets and activity pages to plan your targets.

When my snake is finished, this is what we will do:

....

Finishing date: ....

What a mess!

Share this story with the children.

Poppy's puppies wanted to be good. They really did! They tried to be friends, but somehow things always went wrong.

One morning, Poppy pulled out the toy box and told the puppies to play nicely together, while she was busy. Oscar pounced on the rubber bone. He thought he'd play at burying it. But, while he was busy digging, Pumpkin crept up and grabbed it. 'Give that back!' woofed Oscar. 'I had it first.'

'Too bad!' snapped Pumpkin. 'I want to play with it.'

While they were arguing, Biscuit sneaked towards the bone. 'Bad luck, you two,' he laughed, 'I've got it now.'

All three puppies rushed for the bone. They grabbed, they pushed, they tugged. And they kicked earth all over the lawn.

'What a mess!' barked Poppy, coming round the corner. 'Stop it at once! Choose something you can all play with, without squabbling. Like this.' She nudged a big bright ball towards them. 'I have things to do,' she said, 'but I'll be back in a minute.'

Pumpkin grabbed the ball. 'Hit it to me!,' woofed Oscar. But Pumpkin wasn't going to share. She raced off towards the flower beds. Oscar and Biscuit caught up with her by the daffodils. They snatched at the ball, knocking Pumpkin into the flowers. But she didn't drop the ball, so they followed her, trampling down more of the daffodils.

'What a mess!' barked Poppy, running across the lawn. 'What is the matter with you? Can't you play without fighting? Come and get something to eat. Perhaps that will settle you down.'

The puppies followed Poppy. 'It wasn't me!' they all mumbled.

Poppy pushed three bowls of food towards her puppies. They looked at the bowls.

'There's more in that one!' they all woofed. They charged at the bowl, knocking over the other bowls, as they pushed at one another. They snapped, they snarled, until everyone was in tears.

'What a mess!' sighed Poppy. 'Stop it at once!'

The puppies stopped in their tracks and hung their heads. 'I didn't start it!' they all mumbled.

'No more excuses!' said Poppy. 'You all behaved badly. We need to work out some rules so that everyone can have a turn. The puppies waited for Poppy to go on. 'Everyone can have a say,' she told them, 'Rules will make things fair.'

I wonder what rules they thought of. Do you have any ideas?

Jillian Harker

What rules shall we make up for the puppies?

Why do people need rules?

Try and try again

Oh dear! Things are not going well at Sunnyside School! Can you spot the problems?
How do you think the children are feeling? What should the children do instead?

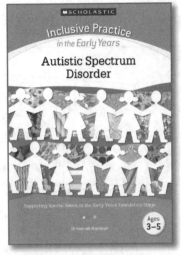

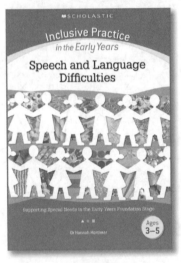
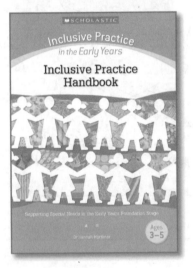